AF651516

An Analysis of Two Lok Sabha Elections in Tamil Nadu

About the Author

Prof. Ganapathy Palanithurai, Rajiv Gandhi Chair for Panchayati Raj studies, Department of Political Science and Development Administration, Gandhigram Rural Institute – Deemed University, Gandhigram is an academic activist working with academic community, civil society, policy community and political community to impress upon them the importance and need of democratic local governance in India to enable the poor to lead a decent dignified human life. All his academic, research and outreach activities are being supported by an array of funding agencies namely the World Bank, the UNDP, the UNICEF, the Hunger Project, SDC, DANIDA, Action Aid International, the Ford Foundation, Population Foundation of India, the Rajiv Gandhi Foundation, Toolkit Foundation Netherlands, Ministry of Panchayati Raj and State Planning Commission. He was a visiting Professor in Cologne University, Germany. He has to his credit seventy three books, 126 research articles, 112 popular articles in popular newspapers, 83 monographs published in a span of three decades. He is the coordinator of UGC-SAP and UGC innovative programme. He held several administrative positions like Dean, Faculty of Social Sciences, Dean, Student's Welfare, Member, Syndicate, Member Senate, Member, and Academic Council in Gandhigram Rural Institute. He was and is member of many advisory committees of the Government of India and Government of Tamil Nadu pertinent to local governance and rural development

An Analysis of Two Lok Sabha Elections in Tamil Nadu

G. Palanithurai

CONCEPT PUBLISHING COMPANY PVT. LTD.
NEW DELHI-110059

© G. Palanithurai

All rights reserved. No part of this work may be reproduced, stored, adapted, or transmitted in any form or by any means, electronic, mechanical, photocopying, micro-filming recording or otherwise, or translated in any language, without the prior written permission of the copyright owner and the publisher. The book is sold subject to the condition that it shall not, by way of trade or otherwise, be lent, resold, hired out, or otherwise circulated without the prior publisher's written consent in any form of binding or cover other than that in which it is published.

The views and opinions expressed in this book are author(s) own and the facts reported by them/her have been verified to the extent possible, and the publishers are not in any way liable for the same.

ISBN-13 : 978-93-5125-145-3

First Published 2015

Published and Printed by

Concept
Since 1974

Concept Publishing Company Pvt. Ltd.
A/15-16, Commercial Block, Mohan Garden
New Delhi-110059 (India)
T: 25351460, 25351794, *F*: 091-11-25357109
E: publishing@conceptpub.com, W: www.conceptpub.com
Editorial Office: H-13, Bali Nagar, New Delhi-110 015, India.

Cataloging in Publication Data—*Courtesy:* D.K. Agencies (P) Ltd. <docinfo@dkagencies.com>

Palanithurai, G., author.
An analysis of two Lok Sabha elections in Tamil Nadu / G. Palanithurai.
pages cm
Includes bibliographical references (pages).
ISBN 9789351251453

1. Elections--India--Tamil Nadu. 2. India. Parliament. Lok Sabha--Elections, 2009. 3. India. Parliament. Lok Sabha--Elections, 2014. 4. Tamil Nadu (India)--Politics and government. I. Title.

DDC 324.954820532 23

To
Divine Mother

Preface

India is called itself a vibrant democratic country on only two counts, namely conducting election periodically and allowing the winners to assume office and run the government. For the past six and half decades democracy exist in form in India and it has got a framework of organizing politics. But it is being contested. On all other substantive aspects of democracy India has got deficit. Researchers who looked at India's commitment in deepening democracy from the western perspective appreciated India more than it deserves as they know India has many factors which would work against democracy. So conducting election and keeping the elected government for a specific period is a great achievement of this country.

For many Indians, general elections are celebrations and festivals. Voters mostly the poor have been mobilized and they have been brought to the polling booth to cast their votes which is called electioneering. In Indian democracy poor participate in the election and the rich, and the middle class participate and influence decision and policy making. It is a truism that Indian democracy is being saved only by the poor by participating in the electoral process actively and they are being mobilized by the political parties and the media. No doubt they are being pushed and pulled. In a democracy from the conduct of election to conduct of the decision making bodies, an array of steps in the process. They fall in both institutional functioning and behavioural aspects of the participants in the institutions and communities. Researchers of late look at the election more from the institutional points of view than behavioural aspects of the people who involve in the electoral process. Who wins, with what margin and the factors behind them are matters much in the main discourse. As a student of democracy one has to look at the process much more than the end product of the election. Because the means decide the outcome and its intensity. Why the process in the conduct of election is so important? The reason is very simple. What all the unfair means adopted in the conduct of election either by the political parties or their candidates will affect substantially the process of governance and administration. In a country like India the deep divisions and differences in the society contribute for identity based politics and thereby political mobilizations are based on narrow consideration. Mobilizing the poor for political participation in our society is not an easy task. It was during the formative years of independence people were mobilized on ideological basis and the cost of political mobilization was very less. But today all political exercises are high cost based and it requires huge money. Office of service becomes office of profit and as a result public affairs become corrupt and rent seeking. Now political parties barring a few emerged as corporate houses and adopted corporate approach in the conduct of the party affairs and approaching the election. Thus the political process and electoral process became problematic and violative of ethical norms and established constitutional norms. As a result violations in politics become a culture. Major violations are being seen in the electoral process. The institutional arrangements established for the conduct of election could not carry out the whole process successfully as the volume of election was huge and the main stakeholders, namely the political parties violate many of the established norms. In this context watching the electoral process and analyzing the whole electioneering become imperative.

As a student of democracy I have closely watched the electioneering in the past two Lok Sabha elections and analysed the same from the perspective of fair conduct of election. The XV and XVI Lok Sabha elections have been analysed and explained. Along with the analysis of the electoral process, a development scheme implemented by the Government of Tamil Nadu is being analysed. The reason for analyzing the scheme is to look at the impact of a development scheme in the electoral process as the scheme is meant for first time voters. Basically, it is an analysis of election in the backdrop of deepening of democracy and strengthening of democratic institutions.

Acknowledgements

I have been always a conscious teacher and researcher. It is because of the orientation I had when I was in Annamalai University. Annamalai University (Not now) in the past was known for building social transformative movements. Since I was oriented and shaped my teachers to be socially aware and concern, I look at issues, analyze the same and finally I act on the issues with a perspective. I can quote an example from my student life. When I was a Research Scholar in the Department of Political Science in Annamalai University, teachers of the University were on strike for their just demands. I saw their demands, and they were genuine and they fought for their just demands. Having seen their cause I also participated in their strike by mobilizing the Research Scholars despite threatening from the authorities. Finally, I was arrested and remanded for thirty days in the central prison in Cuddalore. I was released and I continued my Ph.D. programme in the same university and I got Ph.D. degree also. I got a job in the same university despite opposition from the management because I participated in the strike. I served in Annamalai University up to 1991 and I got a new assignment in the present place the Gandhigram Rural Institute – Deemed University. I have joined in the Gandhigram Rural Institute in April 1991 with lot of enthusiasm as it was a Gandhian institute working for upliftment of the rural masses through its extension activities. When I joined the institute, the entire non-teaching staffs were on strike. I moved closely with them to understand their problems and to sort out the same through the authorities. It was perceived that I was instigating them to intensity their strike. Later, I was asked to go back to Annamalai

University. I went to Madras High Court and got the order quashed and continued till date in the Gandhigram Rural Institute – Deemed University.

I have given the above two events (I have many more such events in my academic life) to indicate how I am in public cause. I am always fascinated to participate in popular mobilization either for political transformations or for social transformation. I am passionate in working with people and writing about them for popular consumption and for research world. I connect myself with grassroots and policy community through my writings. In this journey, I come across variety of people. I moved closely with them for learning and sharing. I write always from the field. I connect the field with theory. I build a perspective for myself to look at issues and act on them. For perspective building I take more substance from M.K. Gandhi. From that perspective I look at issues and act on them.

For the above many helped me throughout my life. My father, my mother, community, academia, political party leaders at different levels, media persons, bureaucrates, my colleagues, researchers, project staff, university officials and authorities have helped in shaping my thought process and actions.

For this work I was helped by many. Mostly media persons, social activists, academics, people involved in the election, as officials, political parties' representatives, respondents of focus group discussion enabled me to write articles on Lok Sabha elections. I have written a lot on elections whether it is a State Assembly Elections or Local Body Elections or Lok Sabha Elections. But my approach and perspective are different from psephologist. I look at the process of election from the perspective of strengthening of democracy. I maintain it in all my writings. Who wins the election is not a subject matter for me. How he or she wins is the subject of analysis of mine.

I have to thank all who have contributed for my writings. Specifically my colleagues, researchers, my university authorities and my family members. They are always with me by encouraging me to write continuously and for which I express my sincere thanks from the bottom of my heart to all those individuals.

G. Palanithurai

Contents

Preface vii
Acknowledgements ix
List of Tables xiii
List of Boxes xiii

1. Introduction 1
2. An Analysis of XV Lok Sabha Election 6
    - Introduction 6
    - Backdrop 7
    - Fundamentals 11
    - Precedents 14
    - 15th Lok Sabha Election 18
    - Conclusion 20

    Appendix 22
3. An Analysis of XVI Lok Sabha Election 41
    - Introduction 41
    - Methodology 42
    - A Brief Profile 42
    - XVI Lok Sabha Election 43
    - AIADMK 45
    - DMK 47
    - BJP, DMDK, MDMK, PMK 48
    - The Indian National Congress 49
    - The Left Political Parties 51
    - Reluctant Politician 51
    - Waves at Crossroads 52
    - Media 52

- Integrated Analysis 55
- Conclusion 60

4. An Analysis of a Development Scheme 63
   - Introduction 63
   - Methodology 65
   - Socio-Economic Background 66
   - Purpose 70
   - Owning Development 72
   - Influencing Factor 72
   - Suggestion to Improve the Scheme 75
   - Conclusion 76
5. Conclusion 79

Bibliography 82

Index 84

List of Tables

2.1 Seats Contested and won in 15th Lok Sabha Election in Tamil Nadu 22
2.2 Seats Contested and won in 14th Lok Sabha Election in Tamil Nadu 22
2.3 Voters Polled in 15th Lok Sabha in Tamil Nadu 23
2.4 Tamil Nadu: General Election 2009 Results 24

3.1 Tamil Nadu Lok Sabha Constituencies Votes Polled in 2014 53
3.2 All India Voting Percentage 54
3.3 Vote's Difference 54
3.4 Votes secured by Political Parties 56

4.1 Details of the participants of FGD 67

List of Boxes

I: Neountouchability 73
II: It is a Good Teacher 73
III: Influencing Factor 74
IV: Emotional Attachment 74

CHAPTER 1
Introduction

In 1900 there was not even a single country in the world operating democracy with adult suffrage. Yet there were twenty five countries followed minimum democracy in the world. But in the year 2000, of the 192 countries, 120 countries have come to electoral democracy. In hundred years span a dramatic change happened in the world to adopt democracy as form of governance. But the democratic practice in all the 120 countries is not the same[1]. Democracy though a contested concept, its adoption vary from society to society because of the understanding of the core meaning of the concept "democracy" by different stakeholders. For its effectiveness, people's awareness, understanding, internalization are imperative factors. While operationalising democracy, perspectives and practices vary according to the level of understanding of people about the principles and practices of democracy. Though it varies from society to society there are certain basic tenets with which democratic practices are evaluated and graded. Of all the tenets of democracy, one important basic aspect is how well citizens are socialized, acculturated, oriented to participate in the political process and more specifically to participate in the electoral process. Are the citizens having freedom to participate without any obstacle in the election? Secondly, how well the electoral process is fair and governed with ethical practices. By keeping the two basic indicators the democratic process of the countries is evaluated. The results show that majority of the countries in the world are in minimal democracy and they are struggling to keep the minimal democracy. Democratic deficit is always in the balance sheet of the analysis of democratic practice in the world.

In this context India is being looked at from different perspectives. Of the perspectives one is purely from the western scholars. They look at Indian democracy with two basic tenets. One, the regular conduct of election and the next the winners are allowed to assume office and run the government. From the westerner's perspective following the above basic two tenets is the biggest achievement as Indian society has more negative factors to democracy. Many had suspicion over the longevity of representative democracy in India. But today the representative democracy is in vogue continuously in India with a small interruption for about two years which dispels the suspicion over the substance of representative democracy. It is a known fact that Indian society is in minimal democracy and it faces the implications of deficit of democracy. Yet it is being appreciated. For the committed democrats in India, even the minimal democracy faces certain limitations because of the unfairness in the conduct of election. It is not only in India but also in many other countries this kind of unfair practice in the electoral politics has afflicted the political process and thereby it affected governance and administration. Even in minimal democracy what is more important is enabling every individual to exercise their electoral rights freely without any resistance. People from all segments have to be enabled to exercise their option freely. It is pertinent to note an important point here that the citizens have to be conscientised on the importance and value of franchise one has to exercise in a democratic country. Many of the countries in the world granting universal adult suffrage are through a prolonged struggle of the people. In the process of the struggle, people get oriented and conscientised on the value and importance of the franchise. India is unique in getting adult franchise as it was given at one stroke. In countries like India people have to be prepared, conscientised and sensitized on the importance and criticality of franchise in deciding the fate of the millions. This preparation has to be done by various actors and more specifically the political parties, civil society organisations and media. All have to work in tantrum. In the last six decades India witnessed huge political mobilization and in the process people could have been conscientised and sensitized on the value of democracy and franchise. As a result they would realize the worth of their votes[2].

In the middle of nineties an academic exercise started in the West to study the electoral system and practices and more specifically the impact of the electoral system in the society. The study group has deeply analyzed the electoral process in more than fifty countries. The reason for analyzing the electoral systems and practices is the fact that the way electoral system is operationalised with the active participation of the different stakeholders determines the practices and processes of governance[3]. The basic assumption is fairness in conduct of election will be reflected in fairness in governance and administration. Unfair means adopted in the electoral practices cannot get a fair government and fair governance. In the process of analysis one can find difference in operationalising the electoral system which is natural.

While analyzing the electoral system, it is pertinent to look at the democratic countries which are having extreme socio-economic inequalities among the collectivities. Electoral politics is being influenced by an array of social forces. Countries which are facing extreme socio-economic inequalities find it different to enable the people who are marginalized to exercise their rights freely. Bringing them to the mainstream political process is a difficult task. Even if they are being brought to the political process, enabling them to exercise their rights is yet another difficult task. In the context of tribalistic political process and behaviour making the marginalized to exercise their rights is uphill task. Hence, it is considered essential that a collegium of forces have to work together to perform the above task of enabling the poor and marginalized to exercise their rights freely without fear. In many of the countries while mobilizing the people intensively and more specifically the poor during the time of election, the marginalized are compelled to toe the line of the people and organisations involved in political and electoral mobilization. Thus the voters sovereignty is lost[4].

There is an yet another issue is so vital not only to participate in the election as voters but also to contest in the election as candidate from the marginalized section and the poor. The election machinery has to see that the cost of participation in the electoral process as candidate has to be at the affordable level of the poor otherwise poor has to obey the order of the rich as the rich meet their expenditure. Thus the election machinery has to see the cost of election from the perspective of the poor.

In the recent years countries have witnessed cash for votes in the general elections. Huge money has been spent for purchase of votes. This has escalated the cost of electoral contest. When this practice is not curbed or checked how elections will be conducted fairly. Hence, it is the responsibility of the election machinery to regulate the political parties and media for the fair conduct of election otherwise election will be conducted in an unfair means. Unfair practices in the election are more only in minimal democracies. It is a general expectation that the political parties, civil society organizations, media, academic institutions have to be involved in awareness creation among the public about the potentials of democracy. Barring a few societies, many of the countries are in minimal democracy because of the wilful neglect of all the institutions and organizations in performing the expected task of awareness building among the masses about the importance and implications of democracy. Even minimal democracy functions with several defects and deficiencies. Thus in a minimal democracy one cannot expect maximum performance unless the quality of electoral democracy is ensured[5]. Democracy in its full form has to act and for which enabling conditions have to be evolved and innovations have to be made in democracy and governance[6]. Generally discourse on democracy takes place only in the formal aspects of electoral system and not on the substantive aspects of the electoral practices. As result electoral system is being run with all maladies. In order to rectify the maladies, weakness and deficiencies electoral reforms are being advocated and to push even electoral reforms the election machinery does not have the will and strength as the power lies elsewhere. Hence, a conscious action is necessary on the part of civil society organizations to exert pressure on the government to reform the entire electoral process. Against this background I looked at the election process of XV and XVI Lok Sabha elections in Tamil Nadu. Two electoral processes have been analyzed. Along with the above a development scheme is being analyzed from a political perspective. As a student of political science and democracy, I feel quality of democracy is being determined only when the electoral process is carried out on a fair means. Winning the election and increasing the margin are not the concern of the students of democracy. How fairly elections are being conducted is the concern of the student of democracy. Hence, I have made analysis of the two Lok Sabha elections from the above perspective. How political parties involved in forming alliance, how they mobilized the masses and how the whole election processes were carried out are being analyzed and conclusions are drawn. In the western countries electoral process is a big science. But in India it is the subject of the psephologists.

NOTES AND REFERENCES

1. Hans-Dieter Klingemann, *The Comparative Study of Electoral Systems*, New York: Oxford University Press, 2012, p. v.
2. Survey Data of Centre for the Study of Developing Societies used by Javeed Alam, "What is happening inside Indian Democracy?" in Rajendra Vora and Subhas Palshikar (eds) *Indian Democracy: Meanings and Practices,* New Delhi: Sage Publications, 2004, p. 80.
3. The Comparative Study of Electoral Systems Planning Committee, *The Comparative Study of Electoral Systems: Final report of the 1995-1996,* Planning Committee, 2008.
4. Strom Kaare, "Voter Sovereignty and Parliamentary Democracy" in Haune Marthe Narud and Toril Aalberg (eds) *Challenges to Representative Democracy: Parties, Voters and Public Opinion,* Bergen: Fagbokforlaget, 1999.
5. T.V. Satyamurthy (ed) *Class Formation and Political Transformation in Post Colonial India*, New Delhi: Oxford University Press, 1996.
6. Robert E. Goodwin, *Innovating Democracy: Democratic Theory and Practice after Deliberative Turn*, UK: Oxford University Press, 2012.

CHAPTER 2

An Analysis of XV Lok Sabha Election

Introduction

It is a million dollar question: "How is it that the ethnic political parties, the Dravida Munnetra Kazhagam (DMK) and the All India Anna Dravida Munnetra Kazhagam (AIADMK) are able to keep the state government in Tamil Nadu alternatively under their fold without giving any opportunity to the Indian National Congress to come back to power even after 42 years?" Are the people of Tamil Nadu not tired of the Dravidian political parties? How do these two political parties, despite belonging to the same ideological tradition, fight against each other and keep power with them? Are they keeping the people in good honour by their performance? Even the Left fort of West Bengal is shaken by the Trinamool Congress and the Indian National Congress combine but the Dravidan fort is not shaken. It is also clear that the two Dravidian political parties are not thriving in their ideology. They moved out of the substantial aspects of their ideological contours long back. This is evident from their alignment with the Bharatiya Janata Party (BJP) one after the other. Some other factors are working in favour of them. The third force the Desiya Murpokku Dravida Kazhagam (DMDK), under the leadership of an actor, Vijayakant, appeared to be emerging as an alternative to both the Dravidan parties, in the absence of the Indian National Congress exploiting the opportunity (people are in need of an alternative to the two) and it bagged 10 per cent of the votes in the general elections. It is a surprise to everyone that the Dravidian forces are thriving in Tamil Nadu politics for more than four decades. It is yet another surprise that, despite a strong alliance formed by the AIADMK under J. Jayalalithaa, favourable conditions to the AIADMK combine due to the issues during the elections, the DMK has succeeded in the elections and retained its primacy in winning more number of seats. The factors that worked for the success of the Democratic Progressive Alliance under the leadership of Mr. Karunanidhi are to be analysed in this article.

Backdrop

It is a well known fact that Indian democracy, even after sixty years of experience after independence, revolves round elections instead of permeating into the society as a culture. Of course, the argument of scholars is that the socio-economic cultural conditions in India will work against the practice and functioning of democracy (Weiner, 1989: 22-23) and yet democracy survives in India very vibrantly because of the practice of elections. But elections predominantly occupy the minds of the people and they are considered the only significant democratic element working vibrantly in India.

All political activities are oriented towards elections. Even this election is conducted only for recruiting representatives to State Legislatures and the National Parliament. But the political parties barring a few, never conduct elections to the party positions. The Election Commission compels the political parties to conduct elections to their party organizations. The political parties have adopted all unethical means to capture power by flouting the established norms and procedures. Thus at the entry itself the political parties commit fraud. It is obvious from the functioning of our political institutions that the socio-cultural conditions and practices have influenced the political institutions (Kaviraj, 1997: 2) and thereby our political institutions and organizations are functioning in an authoritarian and feudal mode. The political activities of the parties never bespeak a democratic culture. All activities are driven and directed and not consciously evolved based on deliberation and discussion. In the place of the king or chieftain the leader really rules and does not lead. The society which had been subjugated for several centuries now struggles to come out from the subject culture. The space left by the British has been fully captured by the elites. Democratizing political institutions is incomplete in India. It has to go beyond political institutions. Indian society has to be democratized. Indian families, socio-cultural institutions are still not democratized. Until they are democratized, one cannot find democratic culture in polity. Indian social institutions are strong and they have influence over other institutions. But anyway an election is a key instrument which keeps democracy alive and active.

People feel that they acquire power only through elections. People feel that they have enough space only in elections to participate and hence make this process tough. No one political party or political leader can say that they will be in power for ever. People have started changing parties, leaders and compositions by their voting when parties and leaders contest in the elections to capture power. Now every election in India is crucial to political parties and the people and it gives lessons and messages to the political parties as they are the prime movers. Sometimes, even political parties are confused by the pattern of voting by the people. India, being a vast country with wide variations and differences in terms of social, economic and cultural conditions, the results and trends of general elections are unique and they are to be seen and analysed nationally, regionally and sometimes sub-regionally and locally also.

In India, from the perspective of the voters, constituencies are not looked at from the domain perspective. In a parliamentary election, national issues have to decide the vote and in the same way for a regional legislature, regional issues will decide and so also for local bodies local issues have to decide. But in India it is not so. Elections cannot be analysed from the national perspectives alone. There are constellations of factors working in the electoral process of Indian democracy. There are many factors which are visible and apparent in influencing the voters (Yadav and Palshikar, 2009). Beyond that there are invisible local and regional factors which deeply influence the electoral outcome but they are not captured by the researchers as they are accessible only to micro observers. Many factors are unexplained and they are hidden which cannot be deeply analysed. In India, neither the voters nor the candidates speak out openly about the real issues which affect the electoral process. Free expression of opinion is the basis of democracy. But in India the people, excepting party men and women, are afraid to express their loyalty and preference.

While reviewing the electoral outcome every party tries to unearth the real factors for its success and set out on its onward march but they are not spoken about openly. People know pretty well which factors worked well and which did not in the electoral process but they do not express it openly. It is only the responsibility of the researchers to unearth the truth. Psepholgists make analyse on the basis of the responses which they have obtained from respondents (voters) but sometimes the predictions come true and sometimes they go against the reality (verdict). Their methodology is scientific and yet the result is faulty. Hence the Indian election is an enigma and a paradox. The unpredictable behaviour of the Indian masses renders has turned the results of scientific analysis faulty. Many elections sprang surprises to candidates and parties. Every election is unique and distinct in terms of process and outcome. In India, people are honoured, respected and valued during elections. People also know pretty well that it is a short lived honour and that they will be treated as beneficiaries and petitioners after the elections. In our country, we have His Excellency or Her Excellency the President of India, Honourable Prime Minister, Honourable Chief Minister and Honourable Ministers, Members of Parliament and Members of Legislatures and most respected officials, but do we have respected citizens? The citizens are the most humiliated individuals in our country. Poor are denigrated because of their poverty. People are respected only during the elections. Hence, people want to show their power only during elections.

On many occasions, political parties and their candidates find it very difficult to manage the voters. Gauging their mood and getting votes from them are not so easy. People are sensitive on certain aspects and political parties will not take risks with those aspects. People can be attracted towards certain benefits of which political parties can make promises. Multiple strategies are needed for political parties and candidates to attract the voters. Election management is a science and an art. Having been trained in getting benefits as beneficiaries, people want to gain something out of this exercise also as political parties and candidates start luring them. It is obvious from the reactions of the voters many times in private chats that the life style of politicians is more or less the life style of the corporate. It gives a sense that politicians get money by any means by using their offices. Hence voters feel that they should give what they earn illegally. As a result "cash for voters or notes for voters" has come into practice (Rao, 2009: Annoussamy, 2009).

Despite all strategies, political parties and candidates have started giving money directly to voters with a view to confirming their votes. In Indian social setting by giving money directly to the voters the party and the candidate can get an assurance from the voters. While giving money one cannot presume that all will vote simply because money has been given. Party men and women will not change their preference because of the money. Non-committed voters may be lured and they will vote for notes. There are arguments that the huge flow of money in every walk of life is due to globalisation. Political parties easily make money as globalisation is on and they go in for giving money to voters clearly indicates the fact that the elected candidates will somehow or other take back the money which they have given to the voters and thereby corruption will be deeply rooted in the system of governance and administration. The volume and quantum of corruption has risen to new heights. The conditions have gone to the level of seeking money from the candidates by the voters themselves. By doing so in Tamil Nadu a new trend has been set that people with money power can alone go in for electoral contest and our democracy now is in the hands of moneyed people. This kind of practice is well designed and well carried out in three southern states in India, namely Karnataka, Tamil Nadu and Andhra Pradesh. South India leads in this practice. It is to be noted here that the above three states are progressive in pushing the agenda of globalisation, liberalization and privatization. It is to be assumed that there is a correlation between globalisation and the quantum of corruption in the electoral process. That is the way elections are conducted. Hence the uniqueness of the 15th Lok Sabha electoral process is being analysed in this chapter. In this chapter no attempt is made to cover the entire country. It is confined only to Tamil Nadu (a province in India). The electoral process was closely monitored by the official observers for independent agencies and by independent researchers. The study focuses more on the processes rather than on the results.

Fundamentals

In India elections are being conducted periodically for the National Parliament, State Legislatures and Local Bodies. The normal assumption is that in the national parliamentary election national issues will decide, in the provincial election for state legislature regional issues will dominate and decide, and in the Local Bodies election local issues will determine the outcome. To some extent it is true. But in India in every election the trend may vary. The context decides everything. In India after the onset of coalition policies, national parties, regional parties and sub-regional parties have begun to join together to face elections. All issues from national to sub-regional level will find a place in the electioneering. It is always a combination of national, regional and local issues. The Members of Parliament enter into the domain of activities of MLAs and Local Body leaders and in the same way MLAs enter into the domain of others. Duplicating the work of MLAs by MPs and MPs and MLAs by Local Body members by both MPs and MLAs made the people to assume that all activities can be carried out by all the representatives. In this way confusion is created by the elected representatives themselves. To what degree national issues, regional issues and local issues determine the electoral outcome is the fundamental question.

In the 1977 parliamentary election, from Kashmir to Kanyakumari, people voted against the Emergency. No other issue stood before this factor. In 1980 people voted for stability, order, cohesion and strong leadership with democracy. Hence, Indira Gandhi returned to power. People had forgotten the excesses of the Emergency in the context of instability and weak leadership. People wanted stability with effective leadership. In the same way in 1984, the general elections, the whole country voted in favour of the Indian National Congress after Indira Gandhi was assassinated. No factor worked against this factor—the assassination of Indira Gandhi. It was a single issue that decided the electoral outcome.

In Tamil Nadu food security or food crisis worked against the Indian National Congress in 1967 and in favour of the Dravida Munnetra Kazhagam (ethnic political party). From 1967 to date the politics of rice is active and political parties are playing their card in reducing the price of rice. At present rice in the open market costs

Rs.50 but in the public distribution system it costs Re.1. Moreover universal public distribution system is followed in Tamil Nadu. Thus, rice politics is sensitive in Tamil Nadu. In 1991 general elections to the Lok Sabha and State Legislature, the assassination of Rajiv Gandhi worked against the same DMK and in favour of the All India Anna Dravida Munnetra Kazhagam (AIADMK), an ally of the Indian National Congress. In 1996 it was corruption which drove out the AIADMK from power and the DMK came to power. Thus there are certain events which decide decisively the electoral outcome. Certain national issues and regional issues decisively played a role. Sometimes, it is a mixture of both national and regional issues. Now it has gone further down. It is a mixture of national, regional and local issues as political parties from national to sub-regional level form electoral alliance and issues of a wide range, from national to local levels find value in the electoral process.

It is a well known fact that in India the provisions of the Constitution are valued and respected by the society as long as their community and social practices as per their community constitutions are not contradicted and contested. Communities and collectivities continue to respect the constitution and the government as long as the constitution and the government grant benefits to the people without touching the social hierarchy practiced by them (Palanithurai, 2007: 9-22). Thus in India a fine balancing act has to be done by the political parties to get the votes of the people. Issues of different segments of the society have to be taken into account while making political promises in the form of manifestoes and accommodating candidates from the varied segments. It is almost drawing candidates from all social segments as enunciated by Arend Lijipart in his consociational democracy (Lijipart, 1989). The conditions that exist in India—presence of hierarchy in social structure, high social conflict, high disparity between the rich and the poor, absence of civic culture, extreme social cleavages, widespread misery and unemployment—are incompatible with the practice of democracy.

Indian representative democracy has its own distinct character as it functions in difficult socio-economic and cultural conditions (Khan, 1989: 34-72). But the continuation of democratic regime in India successively and successfully excepting for two years of the Emergency period attests to the uniqueness of Indian polity and democracy and we require a new framework or theory to explain it. Despite all limitations, India has been categorized as one of the few countries in the Third World that sustain democratic institutions. No doubt it is a functioning democracy but it is not a well governed democracy(Kohli, 1997: 383; Palanithurai, 2009). The success of Indian democracy to-day-relies on the conduct of periodic elections to the National Parliament and State Legislature, which is largely attributed to Jawaharlal Nehru who in fact at one stroke gave franchise to all. It was almost a boon and booster to the poor to decide their destiny.

The election is a propelling engine which transforms the social, economic and cultural conditions of Indian society. Because of elections, the political institutions and the state apparatus are compelled to act on certain areas in society. Even till today the poor are valuable citizens casting votes regularly by which the representative institutions are stabilized. In the whole contour of democracy people, that too poor people, know only elections and beyond elections they do not know much of democracy, governance and development. Despite all limitations India remains an electoral democracy. Scholars, by their own standards, classify the democratic regimes which are successful in the world. From the existing practice and perspective the western scholars' classification is also logical. While making classification and categorization of successful democracies, scholars have in mind four important indicators, namely:

(a) representatives are elected through a competitive election in which many political parties contest;
(b) the political parties, including the opposition, have the right to mobilize public support openly and they have access to the press, freedom of assembly freedom of speech and freedom from arbitrary arrest;
(c) parties in power, if defeated, have to step down and the losers are not punished by the winners arbitrarily; and
(d) The elected governments really exercise powers and make policies and they are accountable to the electors (Weiner 1989: 179).

It is to be noted here that in the context in which election is perceived is important to the people. In India the government is a provider and the people are the receivers of benefits. In this way the government has taken on enormous responsibilities. For all the activities of the individual, community and society, permission and certification by the government is essential. People, whether they are poor or rich, individually, collectively, organizationally and institutionally rely on the support, permission and facilitation of the government. Moreover all essential services are being provided by the government. So totally the people cannot lead a meaningful decent life without the help and facilitation of the government. So every step and act of the government is important to the people. People who are in the process of development rely on the policies and in the same way people who are fighting poverty need the support of the government for their survival and to lead a decent life. In this context, the promises and the assurances of the political parties which are competing in the election to capture the government are important. Beyond promises, direct benefits are being given to the voters to get their votes which ultimately pave the way for corrupt practices in the process of governance. At times when the candidates find it difficult to get votes from the people they indulge in luring the voters by giving tangible gift articles and hard cash. This is not done by all. Some of the candidates have adopted this strategy. But now almost all candidates have started adopting these nuances. Maybe the stakes in elections to the candidates and parties are high due to globalisation and hence candidates and parties have resorted to luring the voters. Political parties have started adopting the corporate approach by which effective partnership is formed and a 'win-win' situation is designed whereby every office of service becomes an office of profit. In the formative years of independence the catch word was serve, sacrifice, suffer and build the nation. The new watchword is serve and prosper. Against this backdrop the 15th general election to Lok Sabha in Tamil Nadu is analysed hereunder.

Precedents

The 14th general election was fought on the issue of fundamentalism and secularism. The United Progressive Alliance (UPA) was formed under the leadership of the Indian National Congress at the national level. In Tamil Nadu, under the leadership of the Dravida Munnetra

Kazhagam, the Democratic Progressive Alliance (DPA) was formed, in which the Indian National Congress was a constituent unit. The UPA at the national level and the DPA at the provincial level emerged victorious. The UPA emerged as the single largest alliance and with the support of the Left political parties, the UPA formed the government at the centre. In Tamil Nadu, the DPA emerged victorious by securing all the 39 seats to the Lok Sabha. So the DMK participated in the Central Government as a major partner. Of the 39 seats won by the DPA and the DMK got 16 seats, the Indian National Congress got 10 seats, the Pattali Makkal Katchi (PMK) got 5 seats, the Marumalarchi Dravida Munnetra Kazhagam (MDMK) got 4 seats and the remaining 4 seats were secured by the Left parties, namely the Communist Party of India (Marxist) and Community Party of India.

In 2004, when UPA was formed, the partners of National Democratic Alliance under the Baratiya Janata Party (BJP), namely the DMK, the PMK and the MDMK came out and joined the UPA. The AIADMK contested in this election along with the BJP as an alliance partner. The DPA under the leadership of the DMK secured 1,64,83,392 votes (57.40%), the NDA under the leadership of the AIADMK secured 10002913 votes (34.84%) and others including small parties and independents secured 22,28,212 votes (07.76%). The DPA secured 23 per cent votes more than the AIADMK and BJP combine. The UPA at the Centre accommodated the DMK and the PMK as partners in the government. The Left parties extended support from outside. The UPA government performed very well in some areas. Loan waiver to farmers, National Employment Guarantee Act, Bharat Nirman, National Rural Health Mission, Right to Information Act, Establishment of Higher Learning Institutions, Sethu Samudhram Project and four lane road projects were the flagship programmes. Every year a report card was presented about their performance. At the state level, through forty government departments, four hundred and thirty schemes were implemented. No state government in India implemented such benefit and welfare programmes for the poor. In the era of globalisation, it is the normal assumption that it will benefit the poor. In Tamil Nadu the government introduced such schemes for the poor.

Despite all these progressive activities of the government the partners of the UPA moved out of the UPA. The reasons for their exit were as follows: (a) fear of an anti-incumbent wave, and, (b) contesting independently outside UPA and securing more seats and then bargaining with the party which claims the majority to form the government. At the fag end of five years, the partners and the parties supporting the UPA both from within and outside came out one by one learning only the DMK and the Indian National Congress with the UPA. The Left political parties withdrew their support to the UPA government when Indo-US nuclear deal was signed by India. The PMK came out at the fag end due to the friction between the DMK and the PMK at the regional level and poor handling of the Sri Lankan Tamil issue by the Central and State Governments. Long before that the MDMK came out from the UPA and it joined AIADMK alliance. This was due to the conflict between the DMK and the MDMK. Thus before the 15th General election in 2009, the DMK alone was left with the Indian National Congress. The DMK roped in the Viduthalai Chiruthaikal Katchi (VCK), a Dalit political party in Tamil Nadu active in supporting the Sri Lankan cause. Practically this party was with the political parties which are taking earnest interest in safeguarding the Sri Lankan Tamils. Yet for political survival it aligned with the DMK because there was no assurance from the AIADMK that VCK would be accommodated in the AIADMK camp. The AIADMK formed a strong alliance in this election with the support of the CPI, the CPI(M), the PMK and the MDMK. Many issues were raised against the Central and State Governments. The AIADMK emerged as winning party to win all the 39 seats as the DMK did in the 2004 elections. The price rise, the Sri Lankan Tamils issue, the corruption in the Information Ministry of the Government of India, law and order problem in the region, frequent power cut, lay off in factories due to the power cut, economic slowdown and its implications in the IT sector and a number issues became as strong issues to attract the voters. It was strongly believed because of alliance arithmetic and the chemistry of electoral issues that the DMK and the Indian National Congress alliance would have to face a setback.

In the DMK, the star campaigner, M. Karunanidhi, was not able to make so many trips in the campaign as he did in the 2004 general elections. Further there was no proper coordination between the DMK and the Indian National Congress. There was yet another issue which rocked the boat—the internal rivalry among the groups in the Indian National Congress. Contrarily the AIADMK supremo J. Jayalalitha mounted a strong campaign and pulled the crowd and made virulent attacks on the UPA and the DPA on their acts of commission and omission. She conducted election meetings in forty places. The media extended a helping hand to the AIADMK camp by projecting the trend positively. But the DMK and the Indian National Congress highlighted all the major achievements of the UPA government at the Centre and the DPA in the State. It was totally a performance appraisal for the UPA and the DPA. In the absence of M. Karunanidhi, his son M.K. Stalin conducted the election tour and he covered the entire state. Many of the meetings were roadside shows. He highlighted the major achievements of the DMK government and the UPA government. All populist programmes were highlighted. His brother M.K. Alagiri, South Zone Secretary, was given responsibility for ten Lok Sabha constituencies. He is known for his organizational ability and election management. He tested his propositions in the by-election in Thirumangalam constituency. It was a fort of the AIADMK. To change the trend several strategies were adopted by the DMK under the leadership of M.K. Alagiri. How notes changed the election trend was seen in this by election, which in turn became a formula. Many surprises were thrown up by the Thirumangalam by-election. Political parties lost their faith in other methods of attracting voters as only money purchased votes. The media gave extensive coverage to this aspect and collected video evidence of notes for votes.

Apart from all the above factors the DMK as a party was well organized. Basically the party is a scientifically organized one. Further it is contextualized in the market era. It is not stuck up in an ideological framework. Though the leader is an octogenarian, his approach is modern, current, attractive, and accommodative and up-to-date. This gave the hope to the party workers that by getting victory for the party in the election, party workers would gain. The party successfully spread the mantra "Serve the party and achieve prosperity". "Serve and suffer" is old and "serve and prosper" is the new watchword coined by the DMK. They followed this logic all through. From the beginning complaints and counter complaints emerged on the issue of giving notes for votes in the 15th Lok Sabha election. Cases were registered. A system was scientifically devised to distribute notes and this was exposed in the press also. It was also exposed that money was demanded by the voters. Further voters demanded more money. Normally political parties and the candidates will spend money for meetings, arches, shows, cutouts, hoardings. This amount was saved because of the conditions imposed on the political parties and candidates by the Election Commission through the code of conduct. But that money was used for direct cash payment for votes.

15th Lok Sabha Election

Against this background the election was conducted. To the surprise of everyone the DMK and the Indian National Congress got 18 and 8 seats respectively and the Viduthalai Chiruthaikal Katchi (VCK) got one seat. Totally the DPA secured 27 seats out of 39. The following observations and explanations are based on the election results which are given in the Appendix. The 15th Lok Sabha election results are also compared with the 14th general election results. They are also given in the Appendix.

In the 2004 election, the DPA secured 57.40 per cent of votes and 39 seats. In 2009 it secured only 42.5 per cent of votes and 27 seats. The AIADMK and its allies got only 34.84 per cent votes and no seat in 2004 and now they got 37.4 per cent of the votes and 12 seats. Despite the exit of several parties from the DMK alliance, it secured reasonably good votes and seats. The DMDK, a new political party, secured 10.1 per cent of votes and thereby it enabled the DMK to win this much of seats, despite all the negative factors. The DMDK party was regarded as the spoiler since it spoiled the victory of several candidates. It spoiled the winning chance of the Indian National Congress in 4 constituencies, the AIADMK in 6 constituencies, the DMK in 3 constituencies, the Communist Party of India in 2 constituencies, the PMK in 2 constituencies, the MDMK in 1 constituency, the VCK in 1 constituency, and the BJP in one constituency. In the same way a casteist party, the Kongu Peravai, spoiled the Indian National Congress in 3 constituencies and the DMK in 1 constituency. It was a well known fact that it is a contest between the DPA and the AIADMK alliance. But the DMDK and the Kongu Peravai fielded candidates. All the candidates of the DMDK and the

Kongu Peravai knew pretty well that they were going to be defeated. Yet they wanted to register that they were also a factor to reckon with. Till the finalization of the candidates the DMDK was in search of an alliance partner. It could not clinch the deal with any major political party. Hence, the party spoiled the chances of many. One has to analyse which factor worked in favour of the DMK and the Indian National Congress combine and the AIADMK and its alliance partners.

The DMK, despite its disadvantages worked with hope since it is a party of committed cadres. It has its own electronic media strength. It has support of the government as it is the ruling party in the state. The populist policies and programmes of the government helped the party in the election. Apart from the state government programmes, schemes and individual benefit schemes, the Central Government's schemes like the NREGA and infrastructure schemes helped the DMK and the Congress combine. More particularly notes for votes worked very intensively. The aggressive campaign with a micro approach brought rich dividends to the party. The DMDK took a strong position accusing both the Dravidian parties about their misdeeds. Since the DMK was a ruling party the DMDK could not alienate votes from the DMK camp. It took away a sizeable chunk of the AIADMK votes. The aggressive play of the DMK cadres, the strong play of notes for votes, weak candidates of the AIADMK, poor coordination among the allies of the AIADMK, luring of the functionaries of the AIADMK by the DMK worked in favour of the DMK. But it was mainly the systematic election work done by the DMK that brought victory to the party. Next to West Bengal and Kerala, Tamil Nadu recorded 73 per cent of polling in this election. Comparing with the 2004 elections it is 12.2 per cent up. This is unique in the whole of India. The CNN and the Hindu group conducted a survey which revealed that people were concerned about the problems of Tamils in Sri Lanka. Apart from the political parties, non-political organizations had conducted series of meetings to galvanize the support of the people to exert pressure on the State Government. The rise of the Tamil population in favour of the Sri Lankan issue gave a hope to the people that the electoral victory would depend on the support extended to the Tamils of Sri Lanka by the political parties. The electoral verdict did not reflect this expectation (The Hindu, 2009). The Sri Lankan

Tamil issue did not play any significant role. From the same survey it was revealed that the poorest sections were inclined to support the DMK alliance because of the populist schemes like distribution of free colour television set, gas stove and cooking gas, one rupee rice per one kilogram, and a number of individual oriented benefit schemes along with National Employment Guarantee Programme, all of which made the poor vote in favour of the DMK and the Indian National Congress. Further 12.3 per cent votes were presumed to have been driven by notes which in turn worked in favour of the DMK, defeating the alliance arithmetic. This formula had been tested in the by-election in Thirumangalam constituency. The same media survey revealed that, excepting the Thevar community, most backward caste and scheduled caste people favoured the DMK this time. Equally the upper caste also favoured the DMK combine. The possible explanation is that the benefits of globalisation have been distributed to the poor through populist schemes by which the poor have been gratified. Normally the market economy favours the rich and the capable. The non-committed votes were driven to the booth by notes through a well organized network of the DMK. The AIADMK retained the women and rural vote banks.

Conclusion

The 15th Lok Sabha elections in Tamil Nadu was a very big surprise to political parties, people and the media. Till the results were announced, parties were in confusion. It was unpredictable who would go with whom. Expectations, calculations and predictions were made. But the whole design was upset. But, while analysing the election results, it is necessary to look at the process of the election. The DMK and the Indian National Congress were at a disadvantage. Globalisation has toppled many regimes in India. The BJP and in Andhra Pradesh Chandra Babu Naidu were the best examples. 'India shining' was the slogan of the BJP and Chief Executive Officer was as the slogan of the Telugu Desam. They were totally defeated because of the negative impact of globalisation. The same was expected to happen to the Indian National Congress and the DMK. But the policies pursued by both the governments, like the NREGA and the welfare schemes of the state government saved the DMK and the Indian

National Congress. Of course, the strategies adopted by the DMK and the luring of the non-committed voters helped the DMK alliance to win the election. It was a combination of factors that worked effectively in deciding the electoral victory. The strong money background of the candidates and distribution of money to voters worked very well. The absence of an anti-incumbent wave helped the DMK to get more seats though its alliance was weak. The increased voting percentage helped the DMK to win the election. One has to wait and see the power of money in the next Legislative Assembly elections.

NOTES AND REFERENCES

1. Weiner, Myron (1989), *The Indian Paradox: Essays in Indian Politics*, (New Delhi: Sage Publications).
2. Kaviraj, Sudipta (1997), *Politics of India* (Delhi: Oxford University Press).
3. Yadav, Yogendra and Palshikar, Suhas (2009): "Ten Theses on State Politics in India" in Sandeep Shastri, K.C. Suri and Yogendra Yadav (eds) *Electoral Politics in India in Indian States* (Delhi: Oxford University Press).
4. Bhaskara Rao, N. (6th April, 2009), "How 'Notes for Votes' dampen democracy", *The Hindu*. Annoussamy David (August, 2009), "Lessons from the 15th Lok Sabha Elections", *South Asia Politics*, Vol. 8: No. 4, pp 14-15.
5. Palanithurai, G. (2007), "Constitutional Laws *Vs.* Community Laws" in G. Palanithurai and V. Ragupathy (eds.), *Community, Panchayats and Governance at Grassroots* (New Delhi: Concept Publishing Company), pp. 9-22.
6. Lijipart, Arend (1989), *Democracy in Plural Societies: A Comparative Explorative* (Bombay: Popular Prakashan).
7. Khan Rasheeduddin (1989), "The Total State: The Concept and its Manifestation in the Indian Political System" in Zoya Hasan, S.N. Jha and Rasheeddin Khan (eds): *The State Political Process and Identity: Reflections on Modern India* (New Delhi: Sage Publications), pp. 34-72.
8. Kohli, Atul (1997), "Crisis of Governability" in Sudipta Kaviraj (ed), *Politics in India*, Delhi: Oxford University Press, p. 383.
   Palanithurai, G. (2009), *Third General Election to Local Government in Tamil Nadu: Expectations and Shocking Realities*, (New Delhi: Concept Publishing Company).
9. Weiner, Myron (1989), *The Indian Paradox: Essays in Indian Politics*, (New Delhi: Sage Publications), p. 179.
10. How India voted Verdict 2009, *The Hindu*, May 26, 2009.

Appendix

Table 2.1: Seats Contested and won in 15th Lok Sabha Election in Tamil Nadu

Sl. No.	Tamil Nadu		Turnout (73%)		Seats (39)
			Seats contested	Seats won	Votes (%)
1.	UPA	Congress	15	8	15.0
		DMK	22	18	25.1
		VCK	2	1	2.4
		Total	39	27	42.5
2.	AIADMK and allies	AIADMK	23	9	22.9
		PMK	6	0	5.7
		MDMK	4	1	3.7
		Left	6	2	5.1
		Total	39	12	37.4
3.	DMDK	DMDK	39	0	10.1
	BJP	BJP	18	0	2.3

Table 2.2: Seats Contested and won in 14th Lok Sabha Election in Tamil Nadu

Sl. No	Alliance and Political Parties		Turnout	Seats 39	
			Seats contested	Seats Won	Votes %
1.	UPA	DMK	16	16	24.60
		PMK	5	5	6.71
		MDMK	5	4	5.85
		CPI	2	2	2.97
		CPM	2	2	2.87
		INC	10	10	14.40
2.	NDA	AIADMK	33	0	29.77
		BJP	6	0	5.07
3.	Others	Parties	102	0	4.44
		Independent	391	0	3.30

Table 2.3: Voters Polled in 15th Lok Sabha in Tamil Nadu

Sl. No.	*Parliamentary Constituency*	*Total Votes Polled*	*Total Electors*	*Poll Percentage*
1.	Thiruvallur	849619	1204209	70.55
2.	Chennai North	659889	1023760	64.46
3.	Chennai South	728113	1176861	61.87
4.	Chennai Central	610352	1000705	60.99
5.	Sriperumbudur	794052	1201237	66.1
6.	Kancheepuram	786910	1060188	74.22
7	Arakkonam	853124	1098645	77.65
8..	Vellore	723529	1010067	71.63
9.	Krishnagiri	752578	1014758	74.16
10.	Dharmapuri	778102	1069612	72.75
11.	Tiruvannamalai	840545	1052587	79.86
12.	Arani	841204	1097870	76.62
13.	Viluppuram	796414	1068171	74.56
14.	Kallakurichi	854955	1106364	77.28
15.	Salem	895554	1171839	76.42
16.	Namakkal	845244	1075525	78.59
17.	Erode	767000	1010079	75.93
18.	Tiruppur	741714	993820	74.63
19.	Nilgiris	709705	1003169	70.75
20.	Coimbatore	824047	1163781	70.81
21.	Pollachi	771479	1017811	75.8
22.	Dindigul	820558	1085696	75.58
23.	Karur	824802	1012920	81.43
24.	Tiruchirappalli	718207	1067144	67.3
25.	Perambalur	832216	1049033	79.33
26.	Cuddalore	749394	986026	76
27.	Chidambaram	869709	1126790	77.18
28.	Mayiladuthurai	799580	1091519	73.25
29.	Nagapattinam	762988	982352	77.67
30.	Thanjavur	807776	1054118	76.63
31.	Sivaganga	775253	1092398	70.97
32.	Madurai	791678	1022421	77.43
33.	Theni	800529	1074931	74.47
34.	Virudhunagar	767653	992063	77.38
35.	Ramanathapuram	777839	1133333	68.63
36.	Thoothukkudi	656163	949153	69.13
37.	Tenkasi	746045	1063777	70.13
38.	Tirunelveli	700788	1059687	66.13
39.	Kanniyakumari	765661	1178047	64.99

Table 2.4: Tamil Nadu: General Election 2009 Results

PC No.	*Constituency Name*	*Winning Candidates*	*Party*
1.	Tiruvallur	Venugopal. P.	All India Anna Dravida Munnetra Kazhagam
2.	Chennai North	Elangovan T.K.S.	Dravida Munnetra Kazhagam
3.	Chennai South	Rajendran C.	All India Anna Dravida Munnetra Kazhagam
4.	Chennai Central	Dayanidhi Maran	Dravida Munnetra Kazhagam
5.	Sriperumbudur	Baalu T.R.	Dravida Munnetra Kazhagam
6.	Kancheepuram	Viswanathan P.	Indian National Congress
7.	Arakkonam	Jagathrakshakan	Dravida Munnetra Kazhagam
8.	Vellore	Abdulrahman	Dravida Munnetra Kazhagam
9	Krishnagiri	Sugavanam E.G.	Dravida Munnetra Kazhagam
10.	Dharmapuri	Thamaraiselvan R	Dravida Munnetra Kazhagam
11.	Tiruvannamalai	Venugopal D.	Dravida Munnetra Kazhagam
12.	Arani	Krishnasamy M.	Indian National Congress
13.	Viluppuram	Anandan M.	All India Anna Dravida Munnetra Kazhagam
14.	Kallakurichi	Sankar Adhi	Dravida Munnetra Kazhagam
15.	Salem	Semmalai S.	All India Anna Dravida Munnetra Kazhagam
16.	Namakkal	Gandhiselvan S.	Dravida Munnetra Kazhagam
17.	Erode	Ganeshamurthi A.	Marumalarchi Dravida Munnetra Kazhagam
18.	Tiruppur	Sivasami C.	All India Anna Dravida Munnetra Kazhagam
19.	Nilgiris	Raja A.	Dravida Munnetra Kazhagam
20.	Coimbatore	Natarajan P.R.	Communist Party of India (Marxist)
21.	Pollachi	Sugumar K.	All India Anna Dravida Munnetra Kazhagam
22.	Dindigul	Chitthan N.S.V.	Indian National Congress

(Contd.)

Table 2.4 (*Contd.*)

PC No	Constituency Name	Winning Candidates	Party
23.	Karur	Tambidurai M.	All India Anna Dravida Munnetra Kazhagam
24.	Tiruchirappalli	Kumar P.	All India Anna Dravida Munnetra Kazhagam
25.	Perambalur	Napoleon D.	Dravida Munnetra Kazhagam
26.	Cuddalore	Alagiri S.	Indian National Congress
27.	Chidambaram	Thirumaavalavan Thol	Viduthalai Chiruthaigal Katch
28.	Mayiladuthurai	Manian O.S.	All India Anna Dravida Munnetra Kazhagam
29.	Nagapattinam	Vijayan A.K.S.	Dravida Munnetra Kazhagam
30.	Thanjavur	Palanimanickam S.S.	Dravida Munnetra Kazhagam
31.	Sivaganga	Chidambaram P.	Indian National Congress
32.	Madurai	Alagiri M.K.	Dravida Munnetra Kazhagam
33.	Theni	Aaron Rashid J.M.	Indian National Congress
34.	Virudhunagar	Manicka Tagore	Indian National Congress
35.	Ramanathapuram	Sivakumar @ J.K. Ritheesh K.	Dravida Munnetra Kazhagam
36.	Thoothukkudi	Jeyadurai S.R.	Dravida Munnetra Kazhagam
37.	Tenkasi	Lingam P.	Communist Party of India
38.	Tirunelveli	Ramasubbu S.	Indian National Congress
39.	Kanniyakumari	Helen Davidson J.	Dravida Munnetra Kazhagam

Parliamentary Constituency: Tiruvallur (2009)

Sl. No.	Name	Party	Votes	%
1.	Venugopal P.	ADMK	372466	43.83
2.	Gayathri S.	DMK	339299	39.93
3.	Suresh R.	DMDK	108797	12.80
4.		OTHERS	14449	1.70
5.		IND	15109	1.77
	Total Votes polled		849619	

Parliamentary Constituency: Chennai North (2009)

Sl. No.	Name	Party	Votes	%
1.	Elangovan T.K.S.	DMK	281055	42.59
2.	Pandian D.	CPI	261902	39.69
3.	Yuvaraj V.	DMDK	66375	10.06
4.	Tamilisaisoundararajan	BJP	23350	3.54
5.		Others	8555	1.30
6.		IND	18652	2.83
	Total Votes polled		659889	

Parliamentary Constituency: Chennai North (2004)

S. No.	Name	Party	Votes	%
1.	Kuppusami C.	DMK	570122	62.25
2.	Sukumar Nambiar M.N.	BJP	316583	34.57

Parliamentary Constituency: Chennai South (2009)

S.No.	Name	Party	Votes	%
1.	Rajendran C.	ADMK	308567	42.38
2.	Bharathy R.S.	DMK	275632	37.86
3.	Gopinath V.	DMDK	67291	9.24
4.		Others	47121	6.47
5.		IND	32863	4.51
	Total Votes polled		728113	

Parliamentary Constituency: Chennai South (2004)

Sl. No.	Name	Party	Votes	%
1.	T.R.Balu	DMK	564578	60.37
2.	Bader Sayeed	AIADMK	343838	36.77

Parliamentary Constituency: Chennai Central (2009)

S.No.	Name	Party	Votes	%
1.	Dayanidhi Maran	DMK	285783	46.82
2.	Mogamed Ali Jinnah S.M.K.	ADMK	252329	41.34
3.	Ramakarishnan V.V.	DMDK	38959	6.38
4.		Others	22405	3.67
5.		IND	10876	1.78
	Total Votes polled		610352	

Parliamentary Constituency: Chennai Central (2004)

S.No	Name	Party	Votes	%
1.	Dayanithi Maran	DMK	316329	61.68
2.	Balaganga N.	AIADMK	182151	35.5

Parliamentary Constituency: Sriperumbudur (SC) (2009)

Sl. No.	Name	Party	Votes	%
1.	BAALU T.R.	DMK	352641	44.41
2.	Moorthy A.K.	PMK	327605	41.26
3.	Arun Subramanian M.	DMDK	84530	10.65
4.		Others	8962	1.13
5.		IND	20314	2.56
	Total Votes polled		794052	

Parliamentary Constituency: Sriperumbudur (2004)

Sl. No	Name	Party	Votes	%
1.	Krishnaswamy A.	DMK	517617	61.39
2.	Dr.Venugopal P.	AIADMK	282271	33.48

Parliamentary Constituency: Kancheepuram (2009)

Sl. No.	Name	Party	Votes	%
1.	Viswanathan P.	INC	330237	41.96
2.	Ramakrishnan DR.E.	ADMK	317134	40.30
3.	Tamilvendan T.	DMDK	103560	13.16
4.		Others	12599	1.60
5.		IND	23380	2.97
	Total Votes polled		786910	

Parliamentary Constituency: Arakkonam (2009)

Sl. No.	Name	Party	Votes	%
1.	Jagathrakshakan	DMK	416243	48.79
2.	Velu R.	PMK	306160	35.88
3.	Sankar S.	DMDK	81814	9.5
		Others	23765	2.7
4.		IND	27167	3.1
	Total Votes polled		853124	

Parliamentary Constituency: Arakkonam (2004)

Sl. No.	Name	Party	Votes	%
1.	Velu R.	PMK	386911	49.88
2.	Shanmugam N.	AIADMK	284715	36.70

Parliamentary Constituency: Vellore

Sl. No.	Name	Party	Votes	%
1.	Abdulrahman	DMK	360474	49.82
2.	Vasu L.K.M.B.	ADMK	253081	34.97
3.	Shoukath Sherif	DMDK	62696	8.6
4.		Others	20564	2.8
5.		IND	26714	3.6
	Total Votes polled		723529	

Parliamentary Constituency: Vellore (2004)

Sl. No.	Name	Party	Votes	%
1.	Kader Mohideen K.N.	DMK	436642	58.38
2.	Santhanam A.	AIADMK	258032	34.50

Parliamentary Constituency: Krishnagiri (2009)

Sl. No.	*Name*	*Party*	*Votes*	*%*
1.	Sugavanam E.G.	DMK	335977	44.64
2.	Nanjegowdu K.	ADMK	259379	34.46
3.	Anbarasan D.	DMDK	97546	12.96
4.		Others	29059	3.8
5.		IND	30617	4.06
	Total Votes polled		752578	

Parliamentary Constituency: Krishnagiri (2004)

Sl. No.	Name	Party	Votes	%
1.	Sugavanam E.G.	DMK	403297	54.51
2.	Nanje Gowdu K.	AIADMK	284075	38.40

Parliamentary Constituency: Dharmapuri (2009)

Sl. No.	Name	Party	Votes	%
1.	Thamaraiselvan R.	DMK	365812	47.01
2.	Senthil R. Dr.	PMK	229870	29.54
3.	Elangovan V.	DMDK	103494	13.30
4.		Others	24938	3.20
5.		IND	53988	6.9
	Total Votes polled		778102	

Parliamentary Constituency: Dharmapuri (2004)

Sl. No.	*Name*	*Party*	*Votes*	*%*
1.	Senthil R.	PMK	397540	55.93
2.	Elangovan P.D.	BJP	181450	25.53

Parliamentary Constituency: Tiruvannamalai (2009)

Sl. No.	Name	Party	Votes	%
1.	Venugopal D.	DMK	436866	51.97
2.	Guru (A) Gurunathan J.	PMK	288566	34.33
3.	Manikandan S.	DMDK	56960	6.78
4.		Others	15078	1.79
5.		IND	43075	5.12
	Total Votes polled		840545	

Parliamentary Constituency: Arani (2009)

Sl. No.	Name	Party	Votes	%
1.	Krishnasamy M.	INC	396728	47.16
2.	Subramaniyan N.	ADMK	289898	34.46
3.	Mohanam R.A.	DMDK	105729	12.57
4.		Others	20900	2.48
5.		IND	27949	3.32
	Total Votes polled		841204	

Parliamentary Constituency: Viluppuram (2009)

Sl. No.	Name	Party	Votes	%
1.	Anandan M	ADMK	306826	38.52
2.	Ganapathi P M	DMDK	127476	16.00
3.	Swamidurai K	VCK	304029	38.17
4.		Others	12794	1.60
5.		IND	45289	5.68
	Total Votes polled		796414	

Parliamentary Constituency: Kallakurichi (2009)

Sl.No.	Name	Party	Votes	%
1.	Sankar Adhi	DMK	363401	42.50
2.	Dhanaraju K.	PMK	254762	29.79
3.	Sudhish L.K.	DMDK	132126	15.45
4.		Others	30736	3.5
5.		IND	73312	8.5
	Total Votes polled		854955	

Parliamentary Constituency: Salem (2009)

Sl. No.	Name	Party	Votes	%
1.	Semmalai S.	ADMK	380460	42.48
2.	Thangkabalu K.V.	INC	333969	37.29
3.	Alagaapuram R. Mohanraj	DMDK	120325	13.43
4.		Others	13009	1.45
5.		IND	47791	5.33
	Total Votes polled		895554	

Parliamentary Constituency : Salem (2004)

Sl. No.	Name	Party	Votes	%
1.	Thangabalu K.V.	INC	444591	59.93
2.	Rajasekaran A.	AIADMK	268964	36.26

Parliamentary Constituency: Namakkal

Sl. No.	Name	Party	Votes	%
1.	Gandhiselvan S.	DMK	371476	43.94
2.	Vairam Tamilarasi V.	ADMK	269045	31.83
3.	Maheswaran N.	DMDK	79420	9.39
4.		Others	72005	8.51
5.		IND	53298	6.30
	Total Votes polled		845244	

Parliamentary Constituency: Erode (2009)

Sl. No.	Name	Party	Votes	%
1.	Ganeshamurthi A.	MDMK	284148	37.04
2.	Elangovan E.V.K.S.	INC	234812	30.61
3.	Muthuvenkateshwaran K.G.	DMDK	91008	11.86
		Others	120459	15.70
4.		IND	36573	4.76
	Total Votes polled		767000	

Parliamentary Constituency: Tiruppur (2009)

Sl. No.	Name	Party	Votes	%
1.	Sivasami C.	ADMK	**295731**	39.87
2.	Kharventhan S.K.	INC	210385	28.36
3.	Dinesh Kumar N.	DMDK	86933	11.72
4.		Others	112150	15.12
5.		IND	36515	4.92
	Total Votes polled		741714	

Parliamentary Constituency: Nilgiris (2009)

Sl. No.	Name	Party	Votes	%
1.	Raja A.	DMK	316802	44.63
2.	Krishnan C.	MDMK	230781	32.51
3.	Selvaraj S.	DMDK	76610	10.79
4.		Others	56424	7.95
5.		IND	29088	4.09
	Total Votes polled		709705	

Parliamentary Constituency: Nilgris (2004)

Sl. No.	Name	Party	Votes	%
1.	Prabu R.	INC	494121	63.26
2.	Master Mathan M.	BJP	257619	32.98

Parliamentary Constituency: Coimbatore (2009)

Sl. No.	Name	Party	Votes	%
1.	Natarajan P.R.	CPM	293165	35.57
2.	Prabhu R.	INC	254501	30.88
3.	Pandian R.	DMDK	73188	8.88
4.		Others	175518	21.29
5.		IND	27675	3.35
	Total Votes polled		824047	

Parliamentary Constituency: Coimbatore (2004)

Sl. No.	*Name*	*Party*	*Votes*	*%*
1.	Subbarayan K.	CPI	504981	57.43
2.	Radhakrishnan C.P.	BJP	340476	38.72

Parliamentary Constituency: Pollachi (SC) (2009)

Sl. No.	*Name*	*Party*	*Votes*	*%*
1.	Sugumar K.	ADMK	305935	39.65
2.	Shanmugasundaram K.	DMK	259910	33.68
3.	Thangavel K.P.	DMDK	38824	5.03
4.		Others	140941	18.26
5.		IND	25869	3.35
	Total Votes polled		771479	

Parliamentary Constituency: Pollachi (2004)

Sl. No.	*Name*	*Party*	*Votes*	*%*
1.	Krishnan Dr. C.	MDMK	364988	56.76
2.	Murugan G.	AIADMK	244067	37.95

Parliamentary Constituency: Dindigul (2009)

Sl. No.	*Name*	*Party*	*Votes*	*%*
1.	Chitthan N.S.V.	INC	361545	44.06
2.	Baalasubramani P.	ADMK	307198	37.43
3.	Muthuvelraj P.	DMDK	100788	12.28
4.		Others	17293	2.10
5.		IND	33734	4.11
	Total Votes polled		820558	

Parliamentary Constituency: Dindigul (2004)

Sl. No.	*Name*	*Party*	*Votes*	*%*
1.	Chitthan N.S.V.	INC	407116	58.92
2.	Jeyaraman M.	AIADMK	251945	36.46

Parliamentary Constituency: Karur (2009)

Sl. No.	Name	Party	Votes	%
1.	Tambidurai M.	ADMK	380542	46.13
2.	Pallanishamy K.C.	DMK	333288	40.40
3.	Ramanathan R.	DMDK	51196	6.20
4.		Others	21444	2.59
5.		IND	38332	4.64
	Total Votes polled		824802	

Parliamentary Constituency: Karur (2004)

Sl. No.	Name	Party	Votes	%
1.	Palanisamy K.C.	DMK	450407	60.43
2.	Palanichamy Ranja N.	AIADMK	259531	34.82

Parliamentary Constituency: Tiruchirappalli (2009)

Sl. No.	Name	Party	Votes	%
1.	Kumar P.	ADMK	298710	41.59
2.	Sarubala R.Thondaiman	INC	294375	40.98
3.	Vijaykumar A.M.G.	DMDK	61742	8.59
4.		Others	108224	15.06
5.		IND	16898	2.35
	Total Votes polled		718207	

Parliamentary Constituency: Thiruchirappalli (2004)

Sl. No.	Name	Party	Votes	%
1.	Ganesan L.	MDMK	450907	63.59
2.	Paranjothi M.	AIADMK	234182	33.02

Parliamentary Constituency: Perambalur (SC) (2009)

Sl. No.	Name	Party	Votes	%
1.	Napoleon, D.	DMK	398742	47.91
2.	Balasubramanian K.K.	ADMK	321138	30.58
3.	Kamaraj Durai	DMDK	74317	8.93
4.		Others	13017	1.56
5.		IND	25002	3.00
	Total Votes polled		832216	

Parliamentary Constituency: Perambalur (2004)

Sl. No.	Name	Party	Votes	%
1.	Raja A.	DMK	389708	55.01
2.	Sundaram Dr.M.	AIADMK	236375	33.37

Parliamentary Constituency: Cuddalore (2009)

Sl. No.	Name	Party	Votes	%
1.	Alagiri S.	INC	320473	42.76
2.	Sampath M.C.	ADMK	296941	39.62
3.	Dhamotharan M.C.	DMDK	93172	12.43
4.		Others	310255	41.40
5.		IND	25494	3.40
	Total Votes polled		749394	

Parliamentary Constituency: Cuddalore (2004)

Sl. No.	Name	Party	Votes	%
1.	Venkatapathy K.	DMK	400059	52.63
2.	Rajendran R.	AIADMK	268707	35.35

Parliamentary Constituency: Chidambaram (SC) (2009)

Sl. No.	Name	Party	Votes	%
1.	Thirumaavalavan, Thol	VCK	428804	49.30
2.	Ponnuswamy E.	PMK	329721	37.91
3.	Sasikumar S.	DMDK	66283	7.62
4.		Others	8858	1.01
5.		IND	36043	4.14
	Total Votes polled		869709	

Parliamentary Constituency: Chidambaram (2004)

Sl. No.	Name	Party	Votes	%
1.	Pommuswamy E.	PMK	343424	46.17
2.	Thirumavalavan Thol	JD(U)	255773	34.38

Parliamentary Constituency: Mayiladuturai (2009)

Sl. No.	*Name*	*Party*	*Votes*	*%*
1.	Manian O.S.	ADMK	364089	45.53
2.	Mani Shankar Aiyar	INC	327235	40.92
3.	Pandian K.	DMDK	44754	5.59
4.		Others	39245	4.90
5.		IND	24257	3.03
	Total Votes polled		799580	

Parliamentary Constituency: Mayiladuturai (2004)

Sl. No.	*Name*	*Party*	*Votes*	*%*
1.	Mani Shankar Aiyar	INC	411160	59.08
2.	Manian O.S.	AIADMK	15469	30.96

Parliamentary Constituency: Nagapattinam (SC) (2009)

Sl. No.	*Name*	*Party*	*Votes*	*%*
1.	Vijayan A.K.S.	DMK	369915	48.48
2.	Selvaraj M.	CPI	321953	42.19
3.	Muthukumar M.	DMDK	51376	6.73
4.	Veeramuthu G.	Others	5123	0.67
5.		IND	14621	1.91
	Total Votes polled		762988	

Parliamentary Constituency: Nagapattinam (2004)

Sl. No.	*Name*	*Party*	*Votes*	*%*
1.	Vijayan A.K.S.	DMK	463389	61.66
2.	Archunan P.J.	AIADMK	247166	32.89

Parliamentary Constituency: Thanjavur (2009)

Sl. No.	*Name*	*Party*	*Votes*	*%*
1.	Palanimanickam S.S.	DMK	408343	50.55
2.	Durai Balakrishnan	MDMK	306556	37.95
3.	Ramanathan P.D.R.	DMDK	63852	7.90
4.		Others	7461	0.92
5.		IND	21564	2.66
	Total Votes polled		807776	

Parliamentary Constituency: Thanjavur (2004)

Sl. No.	*Name*	*Party*	*Votes*	*%*
1.	Palanimanickam S.S.	DMK	400986	56.56
2.	Thangamuthu K.	AIADMK	281838	39.75

Parliamentary Constituency: Sivaganga (2009)

Sl. No.	*Name*	*Party*	*Votes*	*%*
1.	Chidambaram P.	INC	334348	43.12
2.	Raja Kannappan R.S.	ADMK	330994	42.69
3.	Barwatha Regina Papa	DMDK	60054	7.74
4.		Others	13023	1.67
5.		IND	36834	4.75
	Total Votes polled		775253	

Parliamentary Constituency: Sivaganga (2004)

Sl. No.	*Name*	*Party*	*Votes*	*%*
1.	Chidambaram P.	INC	400393	60.00
2.	Karuppiah S.P.	AIADMK	237668	34.60

Parliamentary Constituency: Madurai (2009)

Sl. No.	*Name*	*Party*	*Votes*	*%*
1.	Alagiri M.K.	DMK	431295	54.47
2.	Mohan P.	CPM	290310	36.67
3.	Kaviarasu K.	DMDK	54419	6.87
4.	Dharbar Raja	BSP	3752	0.47
5.		IND	11902	1.50
	Total Votes polled		791678	

Parliamentary Constituency: Madurai (2004)

Sl. No.	*Name*	*Party*	*Votes*	*%*
1.	Mohan P.	CPI(M)	414433	56.01
2.	Bose A.K.	AIADMK	281593	38.06

Parliamentary Constituency: Theni (2009)

Sl. No.	Name	Party	Votes	%
1.	Aaron Rashid J.M.	INC	340575	42.54
2.	Thanga Tamilselvan	ADMK	334273	41.75
3.	Santhanam M.G.	DMDK	70908	8.85
4.		Others	17911	2.23
5.		IND	36862	4.60
	Total Votes polled		800529	

Parliamentary Constituency: Virudhunagar (2009)

Sl. No.	Name	Party	Votes	%
1.	Manicka Tagore	INC	307187	40.01
2.	Vaiko	MDMK	291423	37.96
3.	Pandiarajan K.	DMDK	125229	16.31
4.		Others	25534	3.32
5.		IND	18280	2.38
	Total Votes polled		767653	

Parliamentary Constituency: Ramanathapuram (2009)

Sl. No.	Name	Party	Votes	%
1.	Sivakumar @ J.K. Ritheesh K.	DMK	294945	37.91
2.	Sathiamoorthy V.	ADMK	225030	28.93
3.	Singai Jinnah S.	DMDK	49571	6.37
4.		Others	190323	24.46
5.		IND	17950	2.30
	Total Votes polled		777839	

Parliamentary Constituency: Ramanathapuram (2004)

Sl. No.	Name	Party	Votes	%
1.	Bhavani Rajenthiran M.S.K.	DMK	335287	49.66
2.	Murugesan C.	AIADMK	225337	33.38

Parliamentary Constituency: Thoothukkudi (2009)

Sl. No.	*Name*	*Party*	*Votes*	*%*
1.	Jeyadurai S.R.	DMK	311017	47.39
2.	Cynthia Pandian Dr.	ADMK	234368	35.71
3.	Sunther M.S.	DMDK	61403	9.35
4.		Others	33750	5.14
5.		IND	15625	2.38
	Total Votes polled		656163	

Parliamentary Constituency: Tenkasi (SC) (2009)

Sl. No.	*Name*	*Party*	*Votes*	*%*
1.	Lingam P.	CPI	281174	37.68
2.	Vellaipandi G.	INC	246498	33.04
3.	Inbaraj K.	DMDK	75741	10.15
4.		Others	127617	17.10
5.		IND	15016	2.01
	Total Votes polled		746045	

Parliamentary Constituency: Tenkasi (2004)

Sl. No.	*Name*	*Party*	*Votes*	*%*
1.	Appadurai M.	CPI	348000	48.85
2.	Murugesan S.	AIADMK	225824	31.70

Parliamentary Constituency: Tirunelveli (2009)

Sl. No.	*Name*	*Party*	*Votes*	*%*
1.	Ramasubbu S.	INC	274932	39.23
2.	Annamalai K.	ADMK	253629	36.19
3.	Michael Rayappan S.	DMDK	94562	13.49
4.		Others	50350	7.18
5.		IND	27315	3.89
	Total Votes polled		700788	

Parliamentary Constituency: Thirunelveli (2004)

Sl. No.	*Name*	*Party*	*Votes*	*%*
1.	Dhanuskodi Athithan R.	INC	370127	58.39
2.	Amirtha Ganesan R.	AIADMK	203052	32.03

Parliamentary Constituency: Kanniyakumari (2009)

Sl. No.	*Name*	*Party*	*Votes*	*%*
1.	Helen Davidson J.	DMK	320161	41.81
2.	Radhakrishnan P.	BJP	254474	33.23
3.	Austin S.	DMDK	68472	8.94
4.		Others	96493	12.60
5.		IND	26061	3.40
	Total Votes polled		765661	

Chapter 3

An Analysis of XVI Lok Sabha Election

Introduction

In the last quarter of the 20th century the world has witnessed unprecedented expansion of democracy. Though democracy is a contested concept, the practice of it is in different forms and intensity in the world. It varies from society to society[1]. But the 21st century signalled its consolidation and reformation[2]. The widely accepted form which is not the ultimate finest form is the representative form of democracy[3]. The world is expecting a new refined form but it is yet to come[4]. The practice and processes vary from region to region. Yet the struggle is on for democratization of societies, institutions and organisations and reforming the democratic institutions meant for governance and administration[5]. In this context everyone looks at India a very big political laboratory to test many of the theoretical postulates of representative democracy evolved in the background of the western democracies. Despite the contradiction between the institutional democracy and behavioural democracy and political democracy and social democracy representative democracy in India thrives in form but not in content. The social conditions in India are antithetical to democracy and thereby it leaves room for suspecision of its longevity[6]. Thus studying Indian democracy is always a fascinating exercise[7]. Since it is a biggest democratic country with wide socio-economic cultural variation prompted many to probe into the actual functioning of Indian democracy. While studying Indian democracy one would find large number of scholars concentrating their attention on election related aspects by leaving substantive aspects of it. For many who win with what margin matters much. For a few who are concerned with the quality of democracy, how the whole process of election takes place matter much. Against this background the present work has been undertaken to analyze the whole process of electioneering in the sixteenth Lok Sabha election in Tamil Nadu.

Methodology

Data have been collected from the website of Election Commission. During the election extensively fieldwork has been done through visiting different sensitive constituencies. Closely interacted with media representatives and micro observers. Extensively interacted with party second line leaders and key functionaries. Since I have written extensively on the people's perception of politics, people's perception of governance, administration and development, primary data collected for different projects have been used extensively apart from the published works of the author and others. Election watch group members have been consulted for this work. Some of the opinion makers and editors of monthly magazines have been consulted for writing this chapter.

A Brief Profile

Tamil Nadu is the 11th largest state in terms of its area, 7th most populous state, second largest economy and 6th in India in human development index as per 2011 report. This state sends 39 representatives to the lower house of Parliament which is the fourth highest in India. Of the 39, seven seats are reserved for scheduled caste. The state elects 13 members to the Rajya Sabha. Total number of electorates is 5,37,52,682. Of them 12.5 per cent votes are in the age group between 18 and 25. 49.96 per cent of the electors are women. 60418 polling stations had been set up. Totally 73.67 per cent of voters polled in the 16th Lok Sabha election which is 0.69 per cent increase when it is compared with previous elections in 2009, (72.98%)[8].

Tamil Nadu is forerunner in every event in Indian polity. For the emergence of regionalism, cultural nationalism, state autonomy, introducing welfare schemes, competitive populism, the two Dravidian political parties are responsible. The political parties namely the Dravida Munetra Kazhagam (DMK) and the All India Anna Dravida Munetra Kazhagam (AIADMK) are keeping the ideological background in the backdrop of all their political activities with a view to keep the National political parties away from capturing power in Tamil Nadu for the past forty seven years[9]. At the same time these parties align with national political parties in the process of forming government and facing general elections. In Tamil Nadu the Indian National Congress was in power up to 1967. In the first general election the Indian National Congress could not get majority in the Legislative Assembly. It was in power with full majority only in two periods from 1957 to 1967. In 1967 election it lost power to the DMK because of the price rise that too the price of rice.

XVI Lok Sabha Election

XVI Lok Sabha election in India is unique in many respects. Corruption, black money, and poor governance played continuously in the electoral process in India in the past several elections. But this election has surpassed all the elections in highlighting the issues of corruption and black money to defeat the ruling party in the election. Secondly, the whole election was conducted in the Presidential election model as it is being done in the US. The role of media is unprecedented. The whole election process was media generated and media dominated and calibrated. Ending corruption, establishing good governance and achieving development are the three major points highlighted by the BJP and through the media, the party tried to reach out the masses. Despite the achievements of the UPA, the Indian National Congress failed miserably in the electioneering to face the opposition's attack. Even before the election it conceded its defeat. Never happened in the history of Indian National Congress as it happened in this election that it is wiped out in many of the regions. The prominent leaders gave a shock to the leadership that they declined to contest in the election with the fear that they will face a humiliating defeat. The target of attack was always on Modi by the

Indian National Congress and the Gandhi family by the BJP. For the BJP the 16th Lok Sabha election was a dream project executed as a well conceived business project. In such a way the electioneering of the BJP was designed and carried out. Totally politics and election have been corporatised and marketed sharply.

In Tamil Nadu, 16th Lok Sabha Election brought new equations and experiences of the political parties in the conduct of political processes. The AIADMK has determined to emerge as strong winner with at least 30 seats to play an active role in the formation of new government at the Centre. In Tamil Nadu all political parties have entered into the electoral competition with the assumption that they are going to play a significant role in government formation at the Centre after the election. It was unequivocal from their arguments that they expected a fractured verdict and for government formation their number is significant and important. Of all the political parties the AIADMK wanted to play a decisive role in the new government more than the DMK in UPA-I and UPA-II. The AIADMK target of isolating the DMK from the Congress has been achieved well before the general election. The DMK's perspective framework is to form a formidable alliance by leaving the Indian National Congress and getting the support of the DMDK led by the actor Vijayakanth. The DMK wanted to escape from the anti-incumbent wave and hence it came out from the Indian National Congress. It tried to form a formidable front by taking the support of the DMDK. The DMK kept the Dalit parties and the dominant Muslim parties in tact in its fold. The political parties which were not with the AIADMK have felt that the anti-incumbency wave will hit the DMK also as it was part of UPA-I and UPA-II and many of the misdeeds of the UPA-I and UPA-II. People dissolutioned with the Dravidian Parties were looking for an alternative. The new parties have decided to make use of this opportunity to go with BJP and use Modi's wave for their own advantages to enter into Central Government formation and to reduce the strength of both Dravidian parties. Because the two Dravidian parties, namely the AIADMK and the DMK tried to marginalise the smaller parties in Tamil Nadu. The BJP also considered this opportunity is the finest one to expand its space with the support of these smaller parties like the PMK, the DMDK, the MDMK and a few others. The left parties aligned with the AIADMK initially with the hope to prevent the AIADMK from forming alliance with the BJP and to make it a part of the third front and the left parties were dropped from the alliance later. Hence they were compelled to fight and face the election alone. The Indian National Congress had to go it alone. While forming alliance winning more seats is the only objective and beyond that perspective, ideology and principles had no role to play. Occasionally secularism had been used.

Tamil Nadu is the biggest beneficiary in getting substantial scheme assistance from the Central Government and provided enough infrastructure facilities. It is effectively argued that Tamil Nadu is far better in many of the development indicators. Yet those achievements could not be projected as the DMK and the Indian National Congress as they faced the election independently without having any electoral alliance. Hence what are all the major achievements they made in the last one decade in UPA had not been projected. Partially the Indian National Congress has projected some of the achievements and that too in the last phase of the election.

AIADMK

The AIADMK had started the election campaign along with Narendra Modi. J. Jayalalitha had sensed the mood even before the DMK. She wanted to take the advantage of the anti-incumbency wave against the UPA-II and at the same time she deliberately planned in such a way that Narendra Modi could not take advantage of the anti incumbency wave in Tamil Nadu. Hence, by using the Tamil sentiments, how Tamil Nadu was betrayed by the Central Government during the UP-I and UPA-II on the cause of Sri Lankan Tamils, Tamil fishermen affected in Sri Lankan sea, in giving power to Tamil Nadu, had been highlighted in the campaign. She also made it clear that if she gets clear mandate with 39 seats she will be a formidable force in the Central Government as it could be a coalition government. First, she registered in the voters mind that by electing AIADMK candidates, she will play an active role in government formation and she will be a better and effective leader to deal with Central Government compared to M. Karunanidhi. Her campaign was high volatile campaign with high pitch arguments against UPA-II. In such a way she attacked the UPA-II and M. Karunanidhi and the DMK. Heavy crowd had been pulled by the party organisation to the J. Jayalalitha's meeting all over the state as we have witnessed Narendra Modi's meeting all over the country. In all the meeting she highlighted all the welfare programmes.

This election keeps J. Jayalalitha at the height with a large gap between her and other political party leaders in the state. She was able to get the support of the major caste groups and Muslim in all the regions despite the DMK's alliance with the Muslim parties and Dalit parties. AIADMK defeated the Dalit party leaders. The vote's difference between the AIADMK and the other parties more particularly the DMK has clearly argues that she has commanded huge support from all sections of Tamil society. Three lakh votes difference in two constituencies, over two lakh in seventeen constituencies have clearly indicated the supremacy of the party and more particularly its leader[10]. Because the DMK was not in a position to capitalise the problems faced by the people in Tamil Nadu. Problems like drinking water storage, and frequent power cut, have affected the poor and ordinary citizens. The DMK could have used it to create an anti-incumbent wave against the AIADMK government. These are local issues yet they could have been used by the DMK. They could not as the party was in total disarray. Thought it is not in power at present, its past image is lingering in the minds of the people. The party has earned a very bad name among the people because of 2G spectrum. Apart from the above the party was in the family grip and District units are under the family grip of district secretaries. A party which opposed feudalism in Tamil society established feudalism in politics through its party. As a result people were against the party DMK instead of the AIADMK. Hence this time there is no anger against J. Jayalalitha. In the past three years she launched series of pro-poor schemes which made the poor in comfort zone and hence there is no anti-incumbent wave. In Tamil Nadu, the concept of development will not evoke any response as in many of the indicators Tamil Nadu is far better than many other southern states[11].

From the very beginning Tamil Nadu Chief Minister J. Jayalalitha maintained that she wanted a clear cut mandate from the people to play a decisive role in the Central Government for the benefit of Tamil Nadu and Tamil society in the world. She never mentioned or indicated in any place that she wanted to become a Prime Minister of

India. She maintained that she has to play a decisive role in the Central Government and for which the plight of the Sri Lankan Tamils, fisherman attitude of the Central Government towards the State government along with the issues of corruption. Both Narendra Modi and J. Jayalalitha maintained the same tenor of attack on the Central Government on the issues of corruption. There was no matching leader from the Indian National Congress or the DMK to counter J. Jayalalitha. Corruption should not be an issue in Tamil Nadu as both Dravidian parties have been branded as corrupt when they are in power as there is no formidable forces emerge in Tamil Nadu political scenario. In every aspect J. Jayalalitha's decisiveness paid richly in the 16th Lok Sabha election. J. Jayalalitha had disciplined the party second line leaders to work hard to achieve the target. Everyone in the AIADMK worked in the election with a sense of fear that they have to face tough time if the party does not get adequate seats as they targeted. People started believing that casting vote is equivalent to that of casting vote for Modi as she is going to support Modi to form the government. Opinion maker Cho. Ramaswamy openly appealed that people should vote for BJP candidates and AIADMK candidates.

DMK

The DMK party slowly moved away from the patriarch M. Karunanidhi to M.K. Stalin by taking a decision to sever its alliance with the Indian National Congress led UPA-II. When it took a decision despite the opposition of one faction led by M.K. Alagiri and his sister Kanimozhi, it has given a sense to the people that the party is in deep internal trouble which made the party to come out from the UPA-II under the influence of M.K. Stalin. It was opposed by M. K. Alagiri and M.K. Kanimozhi. When it came out it was under the impression that it can manage the election by bringing the DMDK party under its fold. Till the last minute it waited for DMDK and in between M. K. Alagiri was suspended and subsequently expelled from the party for his anti-party activities. When the AIADMK kept the left political parties out of electoral alliance, the DMK extended invitation to them. But the left have decided to face the election on their own without aligning the DMK. Consciously they have taken decision as it would affect their image because they have to oppose the Congress and support the DMK party which was a part of the UPA-I and UPA-II. The DMK tried to bring more number of parties into its fold but it failed miserably. The whole electioneering was done by M.K. Stalin. From candidate selection to election campaign he was brain, force and future and M. Karunanidhi was only a figure head. Huge crowds had been pulled by the organisation for M.K.Stalin meetings. In all the election campaign meetings he highlighted the failures of the AIADMK government. They were all local issues. The DMK in its functioning has given a feeling to the people that the DMK has come under the control of M.K. Stalin. M. Karunanidhi was only a figure head and beyond that he has no role. Subsequently people got a perception that the party was sinking due to the family fued of the party leader M. Karunanidhi. M.K. Stalin wanted to be the sole leader of the party as J. Jayalalitha in the AIADMK. From the perception of the people M.K. Stalin is no match to J. Jayalalitha. M.K. Alagiri has done many activities and more particularly he has exposed the party by giving interview to the media. As a result the DMK has discredited itself father. When this party boosted itself as it brought huge money from the Central Government to Tamil Nadu through various schemes, the AIADMK leader J. Jayalalitha countered that the DMK leaders are the biggest beneficiaries in all those schemes. Thus the images of the party and its leaders have gone down.

BJP, DMDK, MDMK, PMK

BJP wanted to form an alliance by using the marginalised political parties by the two Dravidian political parties, namely the DMK and the AIADMK. The two main political parties have used them for their own advantage and subsequently they have been marginalised. All these small parties wanted to become an alternative to the two main Dravidian parties. But they could not emerge as an alternative individually. At the same time they work against each other to keep their space in tact. The BJP wanted to make use of this opportunity to expand its space. It wanted to make use of yet another opportunity the Modi's wave. As the DMDK and PMK oppose each other both could not come to terms with the BJP. At the same time they could not find a road map also. Within PMK, there was no uniform view between father and son, and son decided the course of action. The DMDK was openly interacting with the DMK and the BJP for seats till the last minutes. The DMK started declining after the assembly election. In the last Legislative Assembly election the DMDK emerged as main opposition by pushing the DMK to the third position. A fine opportunity was given to the party and its leader Vijayakanth. He could not make use of the opportunity to marginalise the DMK further by his political actions in the Legislative Assembly. In the course of years, party realised that he has no skill, capacity and capability to build the party further to the level of making it as a ruling party. He is always causing damage to the party. As a result seven of his MLAs have moved away from the party. Further he is not an exception in giving space for the family members in the party. No way is it different from the DMK. His wife and brother in law have come to centre stage and control the party. A stage has come to treat him as comedian in the political arena when the BJP entered into alliance with the DMDK. Everyone thought that he has 8 per cent votes. Reality was different. This kind of internal rifts and confusions have pushed the voters to the side of the AIADMK. Before the formation of the front under the BJP leadership, decisive mood has been set in among the electorates. By giving more number of seats to DMDK than others including BJP, how the BJP could be a leader of the front. DMDK's open deal with both party the BJP and the DMK for seats has reduced the image and the respectability. After forming alliance with the BJP, Vijayakanth attacked the DMK as corrupt. Who will believe Vijayakanth?

The Indian National Congress

This party after 1967 could not dream of coming to power in Tamil Nadu government. At one point of time by the effort of Rajiv Gandhi when he was in opposition decided to contest in the assembly election with the solid image of G. K. Moopanar. During that period the party got 26 per cent of votes but could not turn seats. In Tamil Nadu only two general elections the Indian National Congress captured power with majority of seats. It was during 1957 and 1962 elections. The party never involved in introspection why it could not emerge as a strong alternative to the DMK and the AIADMK. In fact the AIADMK has pushed the Congress to the third position. Before the birth of the AIADMK, the equation was between the DMK and the Indian National Congress. After the birth of the AIADMK, it had eaten away the vote bank of the Indian National Congress. Further the party has created a perception that it is interested in capturing power only at the Centre and it never bothered about the future of the party in the state. This kind of perception has created a lethargic attitude among the state leaders of the Indian National Congress in building the party of the grassroots level. Apart from the above groupism in the party has weakened heavily the prospects of the party in winning elections.

In the present election the party leaders from Tamil Nadu believed that managers of the party at Delhi will form some kind of alliance in Tamil Nadu based on the past experience. But it could not happen as the Delhi managers could not reach out to the DMK or the DMDK in time. The Indian National Congress never involved its own regional leaders in alliance formation. It involved the leaders in seat sharing among the factions. Hence, it has been always a Delhi affair. As a result the Indian National Congress was easily managed by both Dravidian parties through the Delhi managers of the Indian National Congress. Either formation of alliance or sharing of seats, the regional leaders of the party have no role. The Central leaders who deal with the regional political parties are managed by the regional political parties. This kind of handling weakened the state unit and state leaders. The Delhi managers of the party have given perception through their dealings that by giving money tickets could be obtained and by giving money alliance could be formed. Managers looking after the state units have done enough damage to the party. As a result the state leader positions have been weakened.

The moment it was known that the party had to go it alone in the election, all the high profile leaders declared that they were not interested in contesting the election. This has created a very poor image of the party among the voters. While campaigning the high profile leaders of the Congress party could not project its achievements as opponents especially the AIADMK supremo J. Jayalalitha and BJP Prime Minister candidate Narendra Modi highlighted the failure of the UPA. It was a low profile campaign of the Congress party. Only for two places Sonia Gandhi and Rahul Gandhi campaigned and in two places unexpected crowd surged to attend the meeting. By seeing the crowd media started projecting the two candidates for whom Sonia Gandhi and Rahul Gandhi campaigned had an edge for winning. Before the polling everyone said if this party gets original 8 per cent votes it will be a great achievement. But everyone predicted the possibility is bleak.

The Left Political Parties

Never the two left political parties speak in one voice in the past. During this 16th Lok Sabha election both moved closer to the AIADMK. They got the support to get their party candidates to win the Rajya Sabha election. Though initially the AIADMK was inclined to go with left, later it decided to become a formidable force by leaving one seat each to the CPI and CPI(M) which ultimately ended in failure in forming electoral alliance between the AIADMK and the left political parties, namely CPI and CPI(M). Hence, the CPI and CPI(M) decided to go it alone. Though they were invited by the DMK, they decided to go alone as spoiler. In fact it was only an electoral ritual exercises and waste of money and human energy for the left political parties. The left political parties should be on people's politics but they also confined themselves to parliamentary politics and as a result they have wasted their energy in election. A large number of cadres, sympathisers, intellectuals have moved away from the left party activities and they remained as silent spectators and not active.

Reluctant Politician

In a classroom discussion students of our Institute (M.A. Governance and Development) have been asked to compare Modi with Rahul Gandhi. One student stood up and said that Narendra Modi comes as a student of business administration and Rahul Gandhi comes as a student of social work. Modi has given a perception to the people that he is a fighting bull. He has shown it in his activities. He projected that he delivered in Gujarat. He is in the race. But Rahul Gandhi has not evinced such an interest as evinced by Modi. Rahul Gandhi has been seen as a reluctant politician. A question is being asked when opportunity was given to him to take up assignments in the Central

Government, he has not taken up. He promised many times that he is going to revamp the party, but he could not deliver. As a result people have come to a conclusion that neither he changed the course of action in the government nor in the party. As a result there is no proper report card for Rahul Gandhi to project that he has delivered.

Waves at Crossroads

The whole country witnessed a wave against the ruling regime which ultimately favoured the BJP to come to power. In Tamil Nadu that wave was countered by the AIADMK's campaign by its leader J. Jayalalitha. J. Jayalalitha in a pointed way focused her attention on the failure of UPA. She had an advantage of dividing the UPA in Tamil Nadu. For a long she tried to drive a wedge between the two parties, namely the Indian National Congress and the DMK. At last she won. As the DMK and the Congress were in the fray separately both have not projected their achievements instead they criticised each other. J. Jayalalitha used all the Central Government schemes effectively for her own advantage. The anti-Congress wave has been used by J. Jayalalitha very cleverly

Media

Today in India media has emerged as powerful institutional mechanism to deliver categorical judgements on issues based on the facts which they have accessed. It has its own strategies to draw the attention of the people towards their channels and newspapers. It evolves a framework to question anybody and any institution and any organisation but no one should question them. They are beyond scrutiny. In such a context media has done different kinds of shows, discourses, deliberations and conducted surveys and so on. For the support of media there are branded intellectuals with ready stock to justify the opinion of the anger of the show. Media rooms are almost war rooms working for a party. Well conceived designs have been created for taking sides and passing judgements over political issues. Never we have seen such corporatization of electioneering as we witnessed in the present election.

Table 3.1: Tamil Nadu Lok Sabha Constituencies Votes Polled in 2014

Sl. No	*Constituency Name*	*Votes*	*Percentage (%)*
1.	Thiruvallur (SC)	1254930	73.73
2.	Chennai North	909383	63.95
3.	Chennai South	1083847	60.37
4.	Chennai Central	816422	61.49
5.	Sriperumbudur	1288392	66.21
6.	Kancheepuram (SC)	1123380	75.91
7.	Arakkonam	1085801	77.80
8.	Vellore	973905	74.58
9.	Krishnagiri	1068925	77.68
10.	Dharmapuri	1101232	81.14
11.	Thiruvannamalai	1063784	79.80
12.	Arani	1092242	80.00
13.	Villupuram (SC)	1064299	76.84
14.	Kallakuruchi	1104862	78.26
15.	Salem	1149020	76.73
16.	Namakkal	1058440	79.64
17.	Erode	1004928	76.06
18.	Tiruppur	1048204	76.22
19.	Nilgiri (SC)	930410	73.43
20.	Coimbatore	1172367	68.17
21.	Pollachi	1009488	73.11
22.	Dindigul	1082059	77.36
23.	Karur	1043909	80.47
24.	Thiruchirapalli	985791	71.11
25.	Perambalur	1027687	80.02
26.	Cuddalore	981742	78.69
27.	Chidambaram (SC)	1086749	79.61
28.	Mayiladuthurai	1024047	75.87
29.	Nagapattinam (SC)	939400	77.64
30.	Thanjavur	1010812	75.49
31.	Sivaganga	1027058	72.83
32.	Madurai	977401	67.88
33.	Theni	1075087	75.02
34.	Virudunagar	1009114	74.96
35.	Ramanathapuram	998986	68.67
36.	Thoothukudi	914630	69.92
37.	Tenkasi (SC)	1015537	73.60
38.	Thirunelveli	960799	67.68
39.	Kanyakumari	989888	67.69

Source: Election Commission of India.

Table 3.2: All India Voting Percentage

Sl. No	Parties	Percentage of votes secured (%)
1.	BJP	31.0
2.	INC	19.3
3.	BSP	4.1
4.	AITC	3.8
5.	SP	3.4
6.	AIADMK	3.3
7.	CPM	3.2
8.	Independent	3.0
9.	TDP	2.5
10.	YSRCP	2.5

Source: Election Commission of India.

Table 3.3: Vote's Difference

Sl. No	Constituency	Votes Difference
1.	Arakkonam	240766
2.	Arani	243844
3.	Chennai Central	45841
4.	Chennai North	99704
5.	Chennai South	136625
6.	Chidambaram	128495
7.	Coimbatore	42016
8.	Cuddalore	203125
9.	Dharmapuri	77146
10.	Dindigul	127845
11.	Erode	211563
12.	Kallakurichi	223507
13.	Kancheepuram	146866
14.	Kanniyakumari	128662
15.	Karur	195247
16.	Krishnagiri	206591
17.	Madurai	197436
18.	Mayiladuthurai	277050
19.	Nagapattinam	106079
20.	Namakkal	294374
21.	Nilgiris	104940
22.	Perambaiur	213048
23.	Pollachi	140974

(*Contd.*)

Table 3.3 (*Contd.*)

Sl. No	*Constituency*	*Votes Difference*
24.	Ramanathapuram	119324
25.	Salem	267610
26.	Sivaganga	229385
27.	Sriperumbudur	102646
28.	Tenkasi	161774
29.	Thanjavur	144119
30.	Theni	314532
31.	Thiruvallur	323430
32.	Thoothukkudi	124002
33.	Tiruchirappalli	150476
34.	Tirunelveli	126099
35.	Tiruppur	179315
36.	Tiruvannamalai	168606
37.	Vellore	59393
38.	Viluppuram	193367
39	Virudhunagar	145551

Source: Election Commission of India.

Integrated Analysis

First and foremost the AIADMK supremo J. Jayalalitha sensed the mood of the people and launched her election campaign first and used the opportunity and turned the anti-incumbent wave against the UPA-II towards her party. During the election period, the DMK party had a setback as internal rift widened in the party. DMK was under the party treasurer M.K. Stalin and he managed the campaign. In AIADMK J. Jayalalitha, in DMK M.K. Stalin, in BJP led alliance, actor Vijayakanth conducted election campaign in the whole of the state. For Indian National Congress G.K. Vasan campaigned the whole state. Narendra Modi, Advani, Rajnath Singh campaigned for the alliance in a few places. Sonia Gandhi and Rahul Gandhi visited only two constituencies in Tamil Nadu. The AIADMK put ministers in charge of constituencies and the DMK put District secretaries and other senior leaders in charge of constituencies. Though Narendra Modi visited Tamil Nadu to use this opportunity, he could not get advantage as electoral pact was not reached among the parties to face the election. Even after the formation of the front under the

Table 3.4: Votes secured by Political Parties

Sl. No.	Constituency	Political Parties Votes Polled													
		AIADMK		DMK (Alliance)		BJP (Alliance)		CONG		LEFT (CPI/CPM)		Others		Total Votes	Percentage (%)
		Votes	%	Votes	%	Votes	%	Votes	%	Votes	%	Votes	%		
(1)	(2)	(3)	(4)	(5)	(6)	(7)	(8)	(9)	(10)	(11)	(12)	(13)	(14)	(5)	(16)
1.	Arakonam	493534	45.45	252768	23.28	233762 (PMK)	21.53	56337	5.19	—	—	11375	1.05	1085801	77.80
2.	Arani	502721	46.03	258877	23.70	252332 (PMK)	23.10	27717	2.54	—	—	49595	4.54	10,92242	80.00
3.	Chennai Central	333296	40.82	287455	35.21	114798 (DMDK)	14.06	25981	3.18	—	—	54892	6.72	816422	61.49
4.	Chennai North	406704	44.72	307000	33.76	86989	9.57	24190	2.66	23451	2.58	60749	6.68	909383	63.95
5.	Chennai South	438404	40.45	301779	27.84	256786	23.69	24420	2.25	—	—	62458	5.76	1083847	60.37
6.	Chidambaram	429536	39.52	301041 (VCK)	27.70	279016 (PMK)	25.67	28988	2.67	—	—	48168	4.43	1086749	79.61
7.	Coimbatore	431717	36.82	217083	18.52	389701	33.27	56962	4.86	34197	2.92	42707	3.64	1172367	68.17
8.	Cuddalore	481429	49.04	278304	28.35	147606 (DMDK)	15.04	26650	2.71	11122 (CPI)	1.13	36631	3.73	981742	78.69
9.	Dharmapuri	391048	35.51	180297	16.37	468194 (PMK)	42.52	15455	1.40	—	—	46238	4.20	1101232	81.14
10.	Dindigul	510462	47.18	382617	35.36	93974 (DMDK)	8.68	35362	3.27	19455	1.80	40189	3.71	1082059	77.36
11.	Erode	466995	46.47	217260	21.62	255432 (MDMK)	25.42	26726	2.66	—	—	38515	3.83	1004928	76.06
12.	Kallakurichi	533383	48.28	309876	28.05	164183 (DMDK)	14.86	39677	3.59	—	—	57743	5.23	1104862	78.26
13.	Kancheepuram	499395	44.45	352529	31.38	207080 (MDMK)	18.43	33313	2.97	—	—	31063	2.77	1123380	75.91
14.	Kanniyakumari	176239	17.80	117933	11.91	372906	37.67	244244	24.67	35284	3.56	43282	4.37	989888	67.69

(Contd.)

Table 3.4: (*Contd.*)

(1)	(2)	(3)	(4)	(5)	(6)	(7)	(8)	(9)	(10)	(11)	(12)	(13)	(14)	(5)	(16)
15.	Karur	540722	51.80	345475	33.09	76560 (DMDK)	7.33	30459	2.92	—	—	50693	4.86	1043909	80.74
16.	Krishnagiri	480491	44.95	273900	25.62	224963 (PMK)	21.05	38885	3.64	—	—	50686	4.74	1068925	77.68
17.	Madurai	454167	46.47	256731	26.27	147300 (DMDK)	15.07	32143	3.29	30108	3.08	56952	5.83	977401	67.88
18.	Mayiladuthurai	513729	50.17	236679 MTMK	23.11	144085 (PMK)	14.07	58465	5.71	—	—	71089	6.94	1024047	75.87
19.	Nagapattinam	434174	46.22	328095	34.93	43506 (PMK)	4.63	23967	2.55	90313 (CPI)	9.61	19345	2.06	939400	77.64
20.	Namakkal	563272	53.22	268298	25.35	146882 (DMDK)	13.88	19800	1.87	—	—	59588	5.63	1058440	79.64
21.	The Nilgirls	463700	49.84	358760	38.56	—	—	37702	4.05	—	—	70248	7.55	930410	73.43
22.	Perambalur	462693	45.02	249645	24.29	238887	23.25	31998	3.11	—	—	44464	4.33	1027687	80.02
23.	Pollachi	417092	41.32	251829	24.95	276113	27.35	30014	2.97	—	—	34435	3.41	1009488	73.11
24.	Ramanathapuram	405945	40.64	286621	28.69	171082	17.13	62160	6.22	—	—	73178	7.33	998986	68.67
25.	Salem	556546	48.44	288936	25.15	201265 (DMDK)	17.52	46477	4.04	—	—	55796	4.86	1149020	76.73
26.	Sivaganga	475993	46.35	246608	24.01	133763	13.02	104678	10.19	20473 (CPI)	1.99	45543	4.43	1027058	72.83
27.	Sriperumbudur	545820	42.36	443174	34.40	187094 (MDMK)	14.52	39015	3.03	—	—	73289	5.69	1288392	66.21
28.	Thenkasi	424586	41.81	26212 (PT)	2.58	190233 (MDMK)	18.73	58963	5.81	23528 (CPI)	2.32	55415	5.46	1015537	73.60
29.	Thanjavur	510307	50.48	366188	36.23	58521	5.79	30232	2.99	23215	2.30	22349	2.21	1010812	75.49
30.	Theni	571254	53.14	256722	23.88	134362 (MDMK)	12.50	71432	6.64	—	—	41317	3.84	1075087	75.02

(*Contd.*)

Table 3.4: (*Contd.*)

(1)	(2)	(3)	(4)	(5)	(6)	(7)	(8)	(9)	(10)	(11)	(12)	(13)	(14)	(5)	(16)
31.	Thoothukudi	366052	40.02	242050	26.46	182191 (MDMK)	19.92	63080	6.90	14993 (CPI)	1.64	46264	5.06	914630	69.92
32.	Thiruchirappalli	458478	46.51	308002	31.24	94785 (DMDK)	9.62	51537	5.23	17039	1.73	55950	5.68	985791	71.11
33.	Tirunelveli	398139	41.44	272040	28.31	127370 (DMDK)	13.26	62863	6.54	—	—	100387	10.45	960799	67.68
34.	Tiruppur	442778	42.24	205411	19.60	263463 (DMDK)	25.13	47554	4.54	33331 (CPI)	3.18	55667	5.31	1048204	76.22
35.	Thiruvallur	628499	50.08	305069 (VCK)	24.31	204734 (DMDK)	16.31	43960	3.50	13794 (CPI)	1.10	58874	4.69	1254930	73.73
36.	Thiruvannamalai	500751	47.07	332145	31.22	157954 (PMK)	14.85	17854	1.68	—	—	55080	5.18	1063784	79.80
37.	Vellore	383719	39.40	205896 (IUML)	21.14	324326	33.30	21650	2.22	—	—	38314	3.93	973905	74.58
38.	Vilupuram	482704	45.35	289337	27.19	209663 (DMDK)	19.70	—	—	17408	1.64	65187	6.12	1064299	76.84
39.	Virudhunagar	406694	40.30	241505	23.93	261143 (MDMK)	25.88	38482	3.81	20157	2.0	41133	4.08	1009114	74.96

Source: Compiled from Election Commission of India Report.

leadership of the BJP, the electioneering was not done by them in a coordinated way.

2009 Lok Sabha election nobody expected that DMK and the Indian National Congress could get 27 seats from Tamil Nadu. The whole atmosphere was favourable to the AIADMK. But AIADMK could not get the advantage of the political environment as the DMDK with its 10 per cent votes worked as a spoiler. Having realised the role of the spoiler, in the subsequent legislative assembly election the AIADMK entered into an electoral pact with the DMDK and formed the government by pushing the DMK to the third place. Last Lok Sabha election was faced by the DMK as a ruling party in the state government. This time it has to face as an opposition party. In this election it has more disadvantages. It could not form a strong alliance with parties with more votes. It could not project its achievements when it is a part of the UPA-II. Because, if they project achievements it has to share blame also. At the same time it could not blame and criticise the Congress party also. Further the inner party rivalry that too among brothers weakened the party in the election. The position of the patriarch of the party was also weakened. Candidate-wise, the DMK fielded very strong persons with heavy money background. The AIADMK candidates cannot match with them in terms of their money power and social respectability. The DMK fielded strong former Central Ministers, industrialists and businessman which was criticised by M.K. Aalagiri. But this formula could not work in the election.

Cash for vote is yet another issue debated publicly during the election. In many places cash was distributed, it was not only the ruling party AIADMK. It was done by all parties wherever the candidate has got money. In the last election the DMK faced the same charge as it distributed huge money and took more seats to Parliament. It only created Thirumangalam formula. Since the media predicted the fact that the DMK may get 8 to 10 seats, the AIADMK identified all those constituencies and worked smarter. One cannot blame the AIADMK alone. It has got one advantage as it is a ruling party, the state government machinery might have been lenient towards the ruling party the AIADMK. This time the AIADMK has introduced and implemented plethora of schemes benefiting the poor which ultimately helped the AIADMK in this election.

The BJP alliance could have exploited the favourable circumstances if it formed the electoral alliance well in advance. Narendra Modi did a candid service and did the campaign in high pitch by touching the vital aspects of the development problems of the Tamil Nadu. First time voters roughly 12 per cent youth were with Narendra Modi. Specifically through a Tamil TV channel, Narendra Modi gave an interview touched vital aspects which are needed for Tamil Nadu for its development. He made it very clear that if he comes as Prime Minister he will help Tamil Nadu for its all round development. But the BJP alliance could not make use of it as it entered into alliance with the DMDK only at the eleventh hour. The Indian National Congress had no face to face the election and it was waiting for alliance partner up to 11th hour. It did not materialise and hence all prominent leaders kept away from the contest. It was kept before the people as sinner. The party could show a brave face even though it has got tremendous achievements for the poor. J. Jayalalitha had used all the opportunities favourable to her party. She marginalised all the parties. Had BJP formed the electoral alliance much earlier before the first visit of Narendra Modi, the fight would have been between the AIADMK and the BJP combine, but unfortunately it did not happen.

Conclusion

In Tamil Nadu there is no wave on either side. As in the previous election, this election polled 73.67 per cent of votes a little 69 per cent more than the previous election. All the political parties have campaigned vigorously. The BJP wanted to make use of Narendra Modi for its expansion through an electoral alliance with smaller parties. It formed such alliance but it could not achieve as it wanted to achieve. The AIADMK is in a very calculated way managed the entire campaign under the leadership of J. Jayalalitha. As Narendra Modi started the campaign for the whole of India J. Jayalalitha did the campaign candidly for the province. There is no anti-incumbency in Tamil Nadu against the ruling party the AIADMK. Further, the continuous pro-poor schemes and programmes kept the poor in good humour. Hence, she swept the election by securing 37 seats out of 39 seats. The victory margin was huge. She kept the AIADMK far away from all political parties in Tamil Nadu in terms of votes secured. In all meetings she made it very clear that she is going to play a major role in government formation. But the reality is different as the 37 seats could not play a crucial role in government formation. The DMK has given a perception that it is sinking because of its internal family rivalry and that affected the party. Apart from the family fued the level of corruption the party functionaries indulged in while they were in power pushed the people towards the AIADMK. It is not because of the party but for the leader J. Jayalalitha. J. Jayalalitha got acquittal in almost twelve cases filed against her by the DMK party. People are best judges watching the economic growth of the DMK party functionaries. All pre-poll survey predicted that it would secure 5 to 9 seats. It failed to secure a single seat. It is a failure for the party but a victory for M.K. Stalin as the party has come under his control. People had deep anger against the DMK and hence people have supported the AIADMK. The DMDK and the MDMK have failed miserably in this election. The PMK though got one seat, its vote bank has been reduced substantially. The Indian National Congress is the worst hit party in the election. Now, it is a politically untouchable party in Tamil Nadu and other regions.

Most of the political parties have come under the control of one leader or one family which is most dangerous to democracy. There is no culture of running the party collectively and democratically. The behaviour of the party leaders is more of a feudal lord. Tickets are decided by only the leader of the party. Even in campaigning the leaders have not allowed the second rank leaders to emerge. Beyond the control of the Election Commission political parties violated the code of conduct. Cash has been distributed. Huge money has been spent for the election by the parties and the candidates. One would find more of violations in the process of electioneering. This culture brings volume of questions on the understanding of people about democracy. At every level one finds violations.

NOTES AND REFERENCES

1. Jean Baechler, *Democracy: An Analytical Survey,* New Delhi: National Book Trust, India, 1998. p. i.

2. Hans-Dieter Klingemann, *The Comparative Study of Electoral Systems Michigan USA*, Oxford University Press, 2009.
3. J.S. Mill, "Consideration on Representative Government" in J.S. Mill, *Three Essays*, New York: Oxford University Press, 1975.
4. Brendan Howe, Vesselin Popovaski and Mark Notaras (eds), *Democracy in the South,* New York: United Nations Univesrity Press, 2010, p. 9.
5. Madhu Purnima Kishwar, *Deepening Democracy: Challenges of Governance and Globalization in India*, New Delhi: Oxford University Press, 2005.
6. Javeed Alan, "What is happening inside Indian Democracy" in Rajendra Vora and Subas Palshikar (eds) *Indian Democracy: Meaning and Practices*, New Delhi: Sage Publications, 2004, p. 78.
7. Rajendra Vora and Subas Palshikar, *Indian Democracy: Meaning and Practices*, New Delhi: Sage Publication, 2004, p. 79.
8. G. Palanithurai, "An Analysis of the 15th Lok Sabha Elections in Tamil Nadu" *Madhya Pradesh Journal of Social Science*, Vol. 14, No. 2, December 2009.
9. John Harriss and Andrew Wyatt, "The changing politics of Tamil Nadu" in *Handbook of Politics in Indian States* (ed), Sudha Pai, New Delhi: Oxford University Press, 2013, pp. 180.
10. P. Ramajayam and Sandeep Shastri, "No Influence of National Issues in Tamil Nadu", *The Hindu*, 24th May, 2014, p. 13
11. Jean Dreze and Amartya Sen, *An Uncertain Glory: India and its Contradictions,* New Delhi: Allen Lane an Imprint of Penguin Book, 2013.

Chapter 4

An Analysis of a Development Scheme

Introduction

Any action of a government improves the standard and quality of life of the people that too the poor, the governance of the political regime can be considered fair and good[1]. The ultimate aim of any government is to enable the people to lead a decent and dignified human life in the society. To achieve the above governments are trying through a combination of actions, namely enacting laws, chalking out policies, evolving development programmes and schemes, and allocating resources. To uplift the poor, welfare schemes with different nature are being implemented by the government as a welfare state. Many of the welfare schemes are almost investment in human being. The investment in human being will be viewed as an investment for growth and development. Ultimately it ends in human growth. But all investments have not brought the expected results as the government expected or targeted. After carrying out plethora of development schemes and programmes, democratic governments in the world have identified the gaps in all those schemes[2]. It was realized that unless the poor, deprived, marginalized are empowered to participate in the process of governance and development it is very difficult to reduce poverty and achieve development for the poor. Hence, it has been decided that governments have to act as a catalyst and the poor should be made as participants[3]. Empowerment and participation are the two factors which are key for transforming the life of the poor. In India, Tamil Nadu is a pioneer in implementing various kinds of welfare schemes. These schemes are viewed differently with different perspectives. Yet the Government of Tamil Nadu has continuously been implementing series of schemes to transform the life of the poor. The schemes targeted individual, groups and communities. Hence, individual oriented, group oriented and community oriented schemes have been evolved and carried out continuously and relentlessly without paying heed to any of the criticisms against the schemes[4]. Impact of many of the schemes could be seen in the human development index of the state. Many of the social welfare schemes enabled the state to secure higher points to reach nearer to Kerala in terms of Human Development. Both Amartya Sen and Jean Dreze have appreciated the social welfare measures initiated by different governments in Tamil Nadu which enabled the poor to come out from poverty and lead a decent human life[5]. At present Tamil Nadu has been considered as a place for innovative welfare programmes and through which the poor and the lower middle classes have been drawn towards the party in power. Arguments have been projected that Tamil Nadu is known for competitive populism and it has influenced all other provinces which have been ruled by the regional political parties. In the whole of India Tamil Nadu has got the highest number of development schemes[6]. Some argue that it is a vote catching technique and some argue that the government relies on the support of the poor and hence they wanted to uplift the life of the poor and for which Government of Tamil Nadu had introduced series of schemes. Of the schemes giving laptop to the students who are pursuing studies in government and government aided institutions is considered as unique and important. It was interpreted that by giving such laptop to the youth who are first time voters will be drawn towards the ruling party. Against this background an attempt is made to study the impact of this scheme in the life and life style of the beneficiaries. This chapter tries to analyze to what extent it helps the end user of the scheme and what will be the impact created in the minds and lives of the beneficiaries. The above study has been conducted through a combination of methods. Data have to be generated through focus group discussion and case study method.

Methodology

It was decided to have a focus group discussion among the beneficiaries in the Gandhigram Rural Institute. The reason for choosing this institute is that this institute has drawn more than 60 per cent of the students from the rural areas and more than 70 per cent of the students belong to marginalized and other backward class groups. Thirteen students have been drawn from different disciplines for discussion. All the students have been drawn from the poorest strata of the society. They were identified and informed that the whole discussion would be on the utility of the laptop supplied by the Government of Tamil Nadu through a scheme. More specifically the changes it created in the mindset of the beneficiaries. Here it is to be mentioned that the idea for conducting a focus group discussion with the beneficiaries of this scheme came as the author witnessed a number of students from other Departments came to the Department of Political Science with the laptop provided by the Government and used the laptops in the premises of the Department as the Department of Political Science has got Wi-Fi facility created through the Ford Foundation project. All the time the students sat in open space, classrooms during free hours used the laptops. It has been witnessed that they have been serious while using the laptops. Many times many thought that the students have been using the laptops only for seeing movies. But the reality is not. Many of them were seriously engaged by using the laptops. This made the author to think of probing the utility and its implication in the life of the beneficiaries. The discussion was conducted in the Department of Political Science from 2.30 p.m. to 5.00 p.m. in the seminar hall. The discussion started from social and economic background of their families. They explained in detail the conditions of their families. Educational background of their parents, income of their families, their perception about the ICT, and its utility, present usage of the laptop given by the Government of Tamil Nadu, hours of usage, purpose of using the laptops, what improvement they have made in the laptops, the details which they stored in the laptops, what they do when their laptop is in disrepair, how they feel by getting the laptop and using the same while they are in their studies, the amount of political influence it wielded, what additional skills acquired to use the laptop, whether it has increased the employability, and what suggestion could be offered to Government of Tamil Nadu to improve this scheme have been discussed while they were engaged in the focus group discussion. All the deliberations have been recorded point-wise by the students themselves. Two and half hour discussion went on consciously. It was lively, passionate and absorbing. It was an involved and an inspiring discourse. During the discussion some of the participants were emotional as it touched their life. Their outpourings could not be recorded as they were. Some took time to record their emotions and feelings and they have handed over the same to the author of this chapter next day.

Socio-Economic Background

All the students are from the economically very poor background ranging the monthly income of their parents from minimum of Rs. 3750 to Rs. 20000. Four respondents' fathers were really coolies working in the farms. A few others are drivers. Their educational background was not sound and they went up to only schooling. Only one respondents father was a graduate. Not even a single respondent said that she could study on their own without the assistance of the government. Everyone stated that they pursued their studies from first standard to the post-graduation only in government institution with minimum of payment. Even to pay the minimum their parents are struggling. Both the respondents and their parents are in struggle for their livelihood and to pursue higher studies. Their parents have determined to enable their wards to pursue higher studies and equally the respondents have determined to pursue higher studies despite difficult conditions. Their economic conditions made them to feel that government has come to their rescue. It is interesting to note that the respondents have informed that their parents are struggling only to enable them to pursue their higher studies and come up in life. Their parents have a clear vision that higher education to their ward means higher opportunity for their wards to come up in life. It is to be mentioned here that the parents and the students have realized the potentials of education in transforming the life of the human being. This understanding and realization has made them to pursue their education and work hard.

Tables 4.1: Details of the Participants of FGD

Sl. No.	*Participants Name*	*Father's Educational Qualification*	*Occupation of Father*	*Mother's Educational Qualification*	*Occupation of Mother*	*Monthly income of the family*	*Place of birth*	*District*
(1)	(2)	(3)	(4)	(5)	(6)	(7)	(8)	(9)
1.	V. Nandhini	V	Carpenter	VIII	Housewife	5000	Manjakuppam (Rural)	Cuddalore
2.	M. Nagajothi	X	Supervisor	V	Tailor	10000	Mogappair (Rural)	Chennai
3.	S. Dinesh	VIII	Coolie	No Education	Housewife	5000	Vedal (Rural)	Kanchipuram
4.	M. Gomathi	—	—		—	—	Mettur Colony (Rural)	Dindigul
5.	G.M. Abinaya	VII	Coolie	X	Tailor	9000	RM Colony (Rural)	Dindigul
6.	A. Sivamurugan	VIII	Driver	No Education	Housewife	3750	Thadicombu (Rural)	Dindigul
7.	A. Shopia Jency Rani	VII	Coolie	No Education	Housewife	10000	Vellodu (Rural)	Dindigul
8.	T. Ramya	XI	Farmer	VIII	Housewife	15000	Combai (Rural)	Dindigul
9.	G. Padmavathi	X	Archagar	X	Housewife	8000	Bharathipuram (Rural)	Dindigul
10.	L. Rajafnisha	B.Sc Maths	Driver	X	Housewife	20000	Begambur (Rural)	Dindigul
11.	A. Brindha Devi	VI	Driver	VII	Housewife	20000	Nagar Street (Rural)	Tirnalveli
12.	S. Suriya	XII	Farmer	No Education	Housewife	20000	Manjampatti (Rural)	Dindigul
13.	C. Vouvanathi Kasthuri	No Education	Coolie	No Education	Housewife	20000	Pethampatti (Rural)	Dindigul

(*Contd.*)

Table 4.1 (*Contd.*)

Previous Experience in using Laptop	*Duration of usage per Day*	*Purpose*	*Improvement*	*Stored items*
(10)	(11)	(12)	(13)	(14)
Yes (others)	4 hrs	Presentations, Movie, Games, Songs, Typing, Download, Photoshop	Presentation, Photoshop, Word, Creativity	Photoshop, Game Graphics, VLC Media, Movies, Materials
No	6 hrs	Presentations, Movie, Games, Songs, Typing, Download, Photoshop	MS office, Photoshop, Friendly with system	Movies, Songs, Games, Photos, Materials, Software
No	4 hrs	Presentations, Movie, Games, Songs, Typing, Download, Photoshop, Browsing	Using System, Browsing, PPT	Study Materials, Family Photos, Songs
Yes (others)	4 hrs	Mail check, PPT, Report writings, Download typing	Enable me to prepare PPT, Report Writing, Friendly with system, Opening Mails	Tally, SPSS, Photoshop, Images, Materials, Movies
No	4 hrs	Net usage, Facebook, Photoshop, Mail checking, Typing, New songs, New software download.	Typing, PPT, Downloads	Images, Tally, Photoshop, Movies, Dictionary, Materials, Games, Google Talk, Songs, Film
Yes	4 hrs	Education, Jobs, TNPSC, UPSC, Latest News, MS Office		
No	4 hrs	MS Office, HTML, Movies, Songs	Typing Excel	Movies, Songs, Pictures
No	4 hrs	Movie, Song, HTML	Typing, Excel, PPT	Movies, Songs, Pictures
No	4 hrs	PPT Download, Photoshop, Games, Mail checking, MS word, Videos, songs	PPT, Photoshop, Materials	MS office Windows, Adobe Reader Dictionary, Songs, Videos, Games, SKYPE
Yes (others)	6 hrs	Materials Download, Songs, Games, Mail checking, Facebook	Prepare report, PPT, Word, using software	Software, Downloads, Songs, Videos, Films, Photos, Games
No	4 hrs	MS office, Painting, Movies, Games	Computer Knowledge	Photo shine, Photoshop, MS office, Songs,
No	4 hrs	MS office, HTML, Movie, Songs	PPT, Typing	Movies, Songs, Images, Photos
No	4 hrs	Games, Typing, Material	To Use system	Materials, Songs

(*Contd.*)

Table 4.1 (*Contd.*)

If any repair occurred	*Is it useful?*	*Is it influence your vote?*	*What you feel when you are carrying laptop*	*Have you undergone any course after getting laptop?*	*Do you feel that you have fine job opportunities?*	*If you think they get votes in society because of this scheme?*	*What further improvements you want?*
(15)	(16)	(17)	(18)	(19)	(20)	(21)	(22)
Nil	Yes	Yes	Proud	No	Yes	Yes	Wi-Fi Software
Nil	Yes	Yes	Proud	No	Yes	Yes	Tablet
Nil	Yes	Yes	Happy	No	Yes	Yes	CD Drive, Net connector
Nil	Yes	Yes	Proud	No	Yes	Yes	Net connector, CD drive
Nil	Yes	Yes	Proud	No	Yes	Yes	Tablet
Nil	Yes	No	Happy	Yes	Yes	Yes	More quality laptops
Nil	Yes	Yes	Proud	Yes	Yes	Yes	IPAD
Nil	Yes	Yes	Proud	Yes	Yes	Yes	IPAD
Yes	Yes	Yes	Happy	Yes	Yes	Yes	Wi-Fi, CD Drive, Web Camera
Nil	Yes	No	Proud	Yes	Yes	Yes	Wi-Fi, CD Drive
Nil	Yes	Yes	Proud	Yes	Yes	Yes	CD Drive, Net Connector
Nil	Yes	Yes	Happy	Yes	Yes	Yes	IPAD
Nil	Yes	Yes	Proud	Yes	Yes	Yes	CD Drive, Net Connector

Source: Computed.

Purpose

Whatever may be the assistance provided by the government, they are to be utilized properly to get advantage of the scheme. In rural reconstruction process plethora of schemes have been evolved and implemented by the governments to reduce poverty and enable the people to lead a decent life. The success rate was not high as expected. Many of the occasions we found the schemes are underutilized and misused. Corruption was rampant in those schemes[7]. Because the schemes were in the hands of the officials and the stakeholders were not able to make their claim rightfully. From this perspective, students have been asked to explain how the laptop is being used. All the participants are in one voice recorded that they created email ID only because of the laptop and they have developed a habit of corresponding with others mostly friends only through email. The respondents have unequivocally said that they have developed an email culture because of the instrument. It becomes an inseparable instrument in their life. By creating this contact, they are in a group of students. It enabled for peer group interaction among their friends continuously. After the class hours they are in computer exploring new things. They saw a new world. They informed that they are connected with the world. A Wi-Fi connection provided by the university is fully utilized to see hundreds of websites. In the whole process of learning they devoted more attention and time only on laptop. They openly admitted that they have learnt more through computers than the classrooms.

Matters related to their subjects of studies are downloaded from different locations and stored in the laptop. For all the subjects they keep reading material in the laptop. It becomes a culture and practice to go into Google for every new aspect of study. When they are in the university they use the laptop maximum level to visit different websites and download all needed materials and store in their laptop. All the students are having materials which are needed to their studies and for their future. Some of the students openly informed that the best teacher according to them is the laptop. Participants made yet another observation which every teacher has to bear it in his or her mind. They said that on subjects, they keep more relevant and updated material for their studies on the subjects than the teachers. Their expectation from the teacher is learning methodology and not information. They get updated information from the websites. They do not require information now. They have informed that they have learnt the art of getting information.

Almost all the respondents expressed that they got certificate in type writing training. They got the training in order to increase the speed of their typing skill. As it is a practice in Gandhigram Rural Institute that students of any programme have to undergo a course in basics of computer usage. In some of the P.G. Programmes students use to undergo two courses on computer. Apart from the above the department of computer science is offering different certificate programmes in the evening. Students who are interested in learning more computing nuances can join such courses. The respondents have utilized all the opportunities to equip themselves in computing skills. Further they informed that they download heavy material from youtube as in youtube materials are available for learning. Material related to personality development, self-development and skill development are being downloaded and they are being used by them very effectively. It is to be noted here that all the respondents are highly motivated students and hence they have used the instruments very effectively. One can easily witness find for development in them.

All the respondents have used the instrument for seeing movies also. They are seeing best films in the world. They told that the best western movies and Hindi movies are seen by them. Highly educative movies they have seen. In their life they have not seen such movies as they have seen movies through internet. Laptop is used much for power point presentation. All the subject assignments are being prepared and typed. Apart from the above it is being used for creation of facebook. As utility increases, the students have picked up new skills and nuances. Some of the students picked up animation skills. They informed that while preparing the curriculum vitae, the skills learnt so far will be packed. Some of the students showed their C.V. and they are very rich. In terms of skills, they are far better than some of the teachers. In such a way they have developed skills by using the laptops. All the reports to be submitted to the teacher, Department and the University are being typed by them. They go out for taking only the print out outside the campus. In this context some of the participants said that they save money. Some others informed that they type project for other students and by which they earn money for their expenses. All works are being carried out by themselves with their laptops.

Owning Development

For many of the development schemes, ownership is a problem. The beneficiaries will not take ownership of the programme and scheme. When government distributes houses to the poor, their maintenance will not be undertaken by the beneficiaries and they expect that they are to be done by the government. Likewise if toilets are being constructed for the poor, maintenance will not be done by them. For many of the development schemes making the poor responsible and as owners become problematic. But this scheme makes the beneficiaries as owners and as a result it is not only maintenance, but also for enriching the instrument by adding newer Programmes and facilities they took responsibilities. They spent money to make the instrument more sophisticated and extensively usable. The beneficiaries have realized the worth of the instrument. Many of the respondents said that if government evolves schemes like this success rate would be hundred per cent. The beneficiary should feel that the scheme is going to benefit him or her. Beneficiary should realize the worth of the scheme and accordingly it would benefit the user or the beneficiary.

Influencing Factor

All populist measures are introduced by different political regimes are intended to attract the voters for the next election. It is being debated extensively on this issue. There is no doubt that the direct benefits to the people will have more probability to draw the beneficiaries towards the benefactor. It means it would draw the people towards the political regimes which deliver such schemes. In this context the question of their loyalty is being asked. Without any reservation all have said unequivocally that they are loyal and inclined to support a leader or a party which was instrumental in bringing such a kind of scheme. Only two respondents said they are not extending their loyalty to the party which has distributed laptops to

Box I: Neountouchability

Of the thirteen students, two students in a very subtle way told that computer literacy and English communication played a very important role in keeping one segment of the society as untouchables. They are neountouchables. "If anybody carries with him or her a laptop, his or her position is very high. They carry some respect as they are technologically equipped and they are in a knowledge world. In the same way if an individual is able to communicate in English he or she feels that he or she will be in the knowledge world. A modern untouchability system has been perpetuated only through this technology and communication. People who have no skill to operate computer and do not have English communication skill are treated very badly among the educated segment of the society. Having seen the plight of the people many tried to spend huge money to learn computer and English communication skill. Where will the poor go for such huge money to procure laptop for their sons and daughters if they are needed. Giving laptop to poor to learn not only computer operation but also to learn communication skill. Hence, it is a path breaking scheme introduced by J. Jayalalitha the Chief Minister of Tamil Nadu. It is almost removing the modern untouchability. People from the poor segment of the society had an aspiration but it is fulfilled only through this computer. In our heart J. Jayalalitha has got a special place. She will be in our heart for ever as she lit the lamp of transformation in our life."

— *Participants observation*

Box II: It is a Good Teacher

"I never heard about languages laboratory. After joining in Gandhigram Rural Institute, I have seen the language lab and its utility. I came to know the software to learn English. My friends helped me to get the software to my laptop and offered me the head phone which they have used for some time. With the help of my friends I have downloaded many lessons from youtube and used it for my learning. For about one year I struggled to learn computer operation. Just like elementary school students I did lot of exercises as they were given by my friends. I used to complete all the exercises given regularly by my friends. In the same way my friends gave exercises for communication skills. My friends helped me to correct the exercises. When I realized the fact that I am learning and my communication skill is improving my struggle becomes a joy. Really I feel the development struggle is a joyful one. Thereby I learnt communication skill. I had the joy of learning when I realize that I am picking up something that is new. It is to be noted that the utility of the instrument depends on the efforts on the part of the beneficiary who got laptop. We have also seen the laptops in the market for sale. Whenever test papers were given back to me I felt that I have improved. That kind of confidence I gained only through this instrument. Hence, I value the scheme of providing laptop to the students. This kind of scheme will make the students more employable".

—*Participants observation*

Box III: Influencing Factor

Photograph of the Chief Minister is pasted on the laptop and hence I was tempted to ask a question to them. Hence, I asked "what extent it will influence you while you are in polling booth?" "One of the students informed that whether photograph is pasted or not, as long as the laptop is with me, it reminds me to be loyal to J. Jayalalitha. The laptop connecting me with the world. It brings volume of information to me. It made me to learn English. I gained self-confidence through this instrument. Now I got confidence that I will get a decent job. I can live on my own. I can help my father and mother. I cannot forget J. Jayalalitha in my life. When I was in the undergraduate college, I was looking at the behaviour of my friends those who were having laptops. They behave as if they were in a different world which is meant for knowledge. They used some technical jargons which were not known to others. At that point of time I felt that I was deprived of the facility because of my economic status. I never had a clue that I am going to have such a technology in her hand. It was possible because of J. Jayalalitha. I not only now but ever I will be thankful to her. Because she enabled me through laptop to reach a status what I wanted to achieve.

— *Participant observation*

Box IV: Emotional Attachment

When the discussion was on, one of the participants vociferously argued that J. Jayalalitha will continue to launch pro-women schemes in Tamil Nadu. When she made the above observation, another participant said that since she is a double beneficiary, she expects more from J. Jayalalitha. Someone said she is not a double beneficiary she is a triple beneficiary. When they are asked to explain how she is a double beneficiary and triple beneficiary, the beneficiary herself offered to explain. She said "I got bicycle from the Government and that is why I was allowed to join higher secondary school as the school was far away from my house. Had I not received the bicycle from the government my parents would not have allowed me to go to higher secondary school which is far away from native village. It was timely that I got the bicycle. I continued my education in the school up to higher secondary because of the bicycle. Subsequently, I got laptop from the same government led by J. Jayalalitha. Now I am in a higher learning institution with a laptop. Now I am applying for a fellowship through a scheme meant for one girl child in a family. Thus I got triple benefits from the government. Bicycle and laptop I got from the state government and scholarship from the central government. Now I have a hope that I can come up in my life on my own. I have a skill, and by using the skill I can earn at least Rs. 15000 per month. My confidence level is high now. I have a feeling that I can lead a decent and dignified life in the society. That much of confidence I have gained and for which the bicycle and laptops were responsible. Both instruments had been provided by J. Jayalalitha. I am emotionally attached with J. Jayalalitha because she only enabled me to continue my studies by providing a bicycle. Only because of the bicycle my family allowed me to go to

(*Contd.*)

Box IV: (*Contd.*)

higher secondary school. Since I completed my school with high marks and I got a laptop I was allowed to come to higher studies. In my life transformation started from owning a bicycle given by J. Jayalalitha. When I started using the bicycle and travelled through bicycle what transformation I got I only know. It cannot be explained. I am a beneficiary no doubt but now I will help others to come up in life and for which light was lit by J. Jayalalitha." When she made such observation she was in tears. After hearing the story nobody will say it is a vote catching strategy.

the students free of cost. It is not the only benefit given by the leader. Along with that many such benefits are being distributed for the poor, women and children. As a result poor are getting series of benefits from this government. When they are asked about their preference, they all said they would support only J. Jayalalitha. Nobody has reservation over this decision. They are explicit in their response. The intensity of their support is directly linked to the magnitude of the benefits they got out of the schemes. In this context there was yet another question posited to them. Their political party affiliation was asked. Every one said they are not members of any political party. Yet their loyalty goes to J. Jayalalitha as she was the creator of this scheme. They further informed that people those who are benefited by this scheme will certainly be loyal to J. Jayalalitha. This is the trend among the youth.

Suggestion to Improve the Scheme

It is one of the best schemes of the Government of Tamil Nadu like providing bicycle to the girl students. The beneficiaries could get benefit out of it. Since it has got a wider scope, these kinds of schemes have to be improved. The respondents have recommended that while giving laptops best instrument could be selected for this scheme. It should have huge capacity to store data. Otherwise data storage equipment can be given along with the laptop. There are students who carry a library with them through this instrument. Further they pleaded that a large number of software which is helpful to the students could be loaded in the system before distribution. For effective maintenance of the system service provider could be located and fixed and the service providers address could be given to the beneficiaries and for the services by the services provides, cost could be borne by the beneficiaries. By doing so a computer culture could be created even among the poor families. As cell phone has created a new communication culture, laptop to the poor will create a new computer culture at the grassroots.

Conclusion

Any decision in any government in a democracy is aimed at keeping the people with the establishment. To reach out the people governments chalk out schemes and programmes which are considered as welfare programmes and schemes. Welfare programmes and schemes will bring many benefits to the beneficiaries. The benefits are of many types. Some are indirect and some are direct. Direct benefit and individual oriented schemes started operating from beginning of 1980 in Tamil Nadu. It has been gradually multiplied. Many of the schemes have created reasonably good impact in the society. Social welfare programmes for the poor will help the poor to come out from poverty and hunger. Tamil Nadu is always a pioneer in welfare programmes and schemes. In this context every scheme and its impact has to be evaluated. Now new methodological nuances are needed for micro studies. Nuanced focus group discussion would enable us to understand many of the deeper issues in the process of transformation of the society.

Giving laptop to students of the government and government aided educational institutions by the Government of Tamil Nadu has been viewed with different perspectives. To understand the deeper implications of the scheme of the government a study has been conducted and that too through a focus group discussion. For the focus group discussion only students from poorest segment of the society had been drawn. In the focus group discussion what have been drawn are given below:

- The increasing deep division between the students who have got access to information technology and English communication skill and the sections of students who are deprived of the above facilities is bridged through this scheme of providing laptop to the students who are in government and government aided educational institutions.

- The students, who have obtained the instrument, have been using the laptop very effectively to develop different types of skills including communication skill.
- The students are totally connected with the world through the facilities available in the educational institutions. The students have developed self-confidence through this instrument that they will make themselves employable.
- Since the higher learning institutions have provided Wi-Fi facilities, the beneficiaries of the scheme have used the benefits at the maximum level as they do not have such facilities in their houses.
- Their work culture has been changed. The instrument brought hope in their life and it made them to work hard to equip themselves. As a result during the day time after attending the classes they used the instrument to see the mails, browse the materials needed to their studies.
- The students have demonstrated that they fully equipped to the level of the market requirements.
- They have combination of skills to declare themselves fully employable even though they are from the social science stream.
- The scheme demonstrated that this scheme is best instrument to make the students coming from the poor families joining the social science programmes more employable.
- As the scheme provides benefits to the students, their loyalty is unequivocally towards the benefactor.

NOTES AND REFERENCES

1. Gerry Stoker. “Governance as Theory: Five Propositions” in *Public Administration: A Reader* (eds) Bidyut Chakrabarty and Mohit Bhattacharya, New Delhi: Oxford University Press, 2003.
2. David Lawson, David Hulme, Imran Martin and Karen Moore, (eds) *What Works for the Poorest?* Warwickshive: Practical Action Publishing, 2010. pp. 1-25.
3. Bidyut Chakrabarty and Mohit Bhattacharya, (eds) *Administrative Change and Innovation: A Reader*, New Delhi: Oxford University Press, 2005, pp. 245-256.

4. G. Palanithurai, *Rural Development Scenario: A Qualitative Assessment for Action in Tamil Nadu* (Monograph) Gandhigram: Rajiv Gandhi Chair for Panchayati Raj Studies, 2010.
5. Jean Dreze and Amartya Sen, *An Uncertain Glory: India and its Contradiction,* New Delhi: Allen Lane and Imprint of Penguin Books, 2013, pp. 77.
6. G. Palanithurai, *Panchayati Raj System in Tamil Nadu: Act, Rules, and Schemes (In Tamil)* Chennai: South Vision, 2009.
7. G. Palanithurai, "Corruption at Micro Level and Ways to Contain" in *Corruption at the Grassroots: The Shades and Shadows* (eds), N. Narayanasamy, M.P. Boraian and M.A. Jayaraju, New Delhi: Concept Publishing Company, 2000, pp. 169-180.

CHAPTER 5
Conclusion

It is a study of the practices and process of Lok Sabha elections held in Tamil Nadu in the year 2009 and 2014. Attention was paid on XV and XVI General Elections to Lok Sabha. How the process and practices were conducted have been studied. Tamil Nadu is known for its innovative politics. Newer demands, newer perspectives have been built only in Tamil Nadu. Hence, political mobilizations are intense and deep. The main competition is between the DMK and the AIADMK. All other political parties are not major parties as the DMK and the AIADMK. Ideologically these two political parties have no difference. Yet they fight against each other to win election. In simple term these two political parties carried out the politics in Tamil Nadu based on personalities, namely the leaders of the two respective political parties. When M.G.R. was alive it was between M.G. Ramachandran *versus* M. Karunanidhi. After the death of M.G. Ramachandran, it was between J. Jayalalitha *versus* M. Karunanidhi. In a democratic culture there is no room for developing anger and conflict and it will be against democracy. But in Tamil Nadu politics of these two political parties have developed a new political culture to look at each other as arch rivals and enemies. It is politics of vendetta. In such a way political orientations were given to party cadres. Both political parties are leader centric parties. Activities are centring around the leaders. Democratic practice is in form to satisfy the constitutional requirement. The executive and general body meetings held periodically. Deliberation, debate, arguments and discourse never take place. Electoral alliances are formed based on the winability and the preference of the party leaders.

Of the two political parties, the DMK has accommodated the second level leaders in the decision making process whereas in AIADMK it is only the leader of the party. In the electoral process, the whole election cost has been made costlier because of the extensive initiatives to woo the voters through all means. The DMK and the AIADMK have adopted cinematic approach in mobilizing the people. The cost of politics has been increased because of the approach of the two political parties. Both parties adopted the same approach. In both parties leaders role, their perception, decision making, matters much. Both parties have adopted business approach to attract voters. Populist approaches are the base of these parties. In electioneering the two leaders campaign are primary. In the earlier days in all political parties leaders at different levels involved in the election campaign and public meetings. Now it was like the American presidential election, both leaders visited whole of Tamil Nadu. Important cities have been selected for campaign meeting, people are being mobilized by investing huge cost to show the crowd. Target approach has been the perspective of two political parties. Each district is allotted to a person who may be a minister if it is a ruling party or the district secretary, if it is in opposition. Both parties are adopting the same approach.

Election expenditure of both parties is very high if they are assessed realistically. The DMK is competing with the AIADMK and *vice versa*. The total space has been occupied by both the parties. Never the two parties have provided opportunity for other political parties to emerge as an alternative. It was tried only in the XVI Lok Sabha election. The BJP tried through the DMDK, the MDMK and the PMK by forgoing an alliance. The two political parties were alliance partners of both the Indian National Congress and the BJP. The DMK was with any political formation to be in power at the Centre. Both parties are known for competitive populism. The two parties are the role model for the rest of India to announce individual oriented benefit schemes. Both parties target the first time voters. Electoral alliance and image building and individual oriented benefit schemes have helped both parties. Many tried alternative to these two political parties in the past and they could not succeed. In the XVI Lok Sabha election the BJP tried through smaller parties to form an alternative front with the Modi's wave. It could not succeed. One could see 70 per cent participation in the election. Political parties have intensively mobilized the people for the election. The ways and means adopted are not in the lines of the democratic value framework. In democracy decision-making is through a process of consultations and debates. But that culture has been changed. Now Tamil Nadu politics becomes leader centric except a few political parties. In a democracy leaders are assuming the rulership by acquiring authoritarian behavioural traits. Simply because of the fact that elections are conducted we argue that we are in democracy. While looking to the practice of democracy one would find more of authoritarian tendencies in political parties. Election becomes a commercial venture of investing money and taking the same if the party in which investment is made, comes to power. Winning elections and making profits in the process of governance and administration are order of the day.

Bibliography

Baechler, Jean, *Democracy: An Analytical Survey*, New Delhi: National Book Trust, India, 1998.

Bhaskara Rao, N., "How 'Notes for Votes' Dampen Democracy", *The Hindu*, 6th April, 2009.

Brendan Howe, Vesselin Popovaski and Mark Notaras (eds), *Democracy in the South*, New York: United Nations Univesrity Press, 2010.

Chakrabarty, Bidyut and Bhattacharya Mohit, (eds), *Administrative Change and Innovation: A Reader*, New Delhi: Oxford University Press, 2005.

David, Annoussamy, "Lessons from the 15th Lok Sabha Elections", *South Asia Politics*, Vol. 8: No. 4, August, 2009.

David Lawson, David Hulme, Imran Martin and Karen Moore, (eds) *What Works for the Poorest?* Warwickshive: Practical Action Publishing, 2010.

Dreze Jean and Sen Amartya, *An Uncertain Glory: India and its Contradiction*, New Delhi: Allen Lane and Imprint of Penguin Books, 2013.

Hans-Dieter Klingemann, *The Comparative Study of Electoral Systems Michigan USA:* Oxford University Press, 2009.

How India voted Verdict 2009, *The Hindu*, May 26, 2009.

Javeed Alan, "What is happening inside Indian Democracy" in Rajendra Vora and Subas Palshikar (eds), *Indian Democracy: Meaning and Practices*, New Delhi: Sage Publications, 2004.

John Harriss and Andrew Wyatt, "The Changing Politics of Tamil Nadu" in *Handbook of Politics in Indian States* (ed) Sudha Pai, New Delhi: Oxford University Press, 2013.

Kaviraj, Sudipta, *Politics of India* Delhi: Oxford University Press, 1997.

Khan, Rasheeduddin, "The Total State: The Concept and its Manifestation in the Indian Political System" in Zoya Hasan, S.N. Jha and Rasheeddin Khan (eds), *The State Political Process and Identity: Reflections on Modern India*, New Delhi: Sage Publications, 1989.

Kohli, Atul, "Crisis of Governability" in Sudipta Kaviraj (ed.), *Politics in India*, Delhi: Oxford University Press, 1997.

Lijipart, Arend *Democracy in Plural Societies: A Comparative Explorative*, Bombay: Popular Prakashan, 1989.

Madhu Purnima Kishwar, *Deepening Democracy: Challenges of Governance and Globalization in India*, New Delhi: Oxford University Press, 2005.

Mill, J.S. "Consideration on Representative Government" in J.S. Mill, *Three Essays*, New York: Oxford University Press, 1975.

Palanithurai, G. "An Analysis of the 15th Lok Sabha Elections in Tamil Nadu", *Madhya Pradesh Journal of Social Science*, Vol. 14: No. 2, December, 2009.

Palanithurai, G., "Corruption at Micro Level and Ways to Contain" in *Corruption at the Grassroots: The Shades and Shadows* (eds), N. Narayanasamy, M.P. Boraian and M.A. Jayaraju, New Delhi: Concept Publishing Company, 2000.

Palanithurai, G., *Panchayati Raj System in Tamil Nadu: Act, Rules, and Schemes (In Tamil)*, Chennai: South Vision, 2009.

Palanithurai, G., *Rural Development Scenario: A Qualitative Assessment for Action in Tamil Nadu* (Monograph), Gandhigram: Rajiv Gandhi Chair for Panchayati Raj Studies, 2010.

Palanithurai, G., "Constitutional Laws Vs Community Laws" in G. Palanithurai and V. Ragupathy (eds.), *Community, Panchayats and Governance at Grassroots*, New Delhi: Concept Publishing Company, 2007.

Palanithurai, G., *Third General Election to Local Government in Tamil Nadu: Expectations and Shocking Realities*, New Delhi: Concept Publishing Company, 2009.

Ramajayam, P. and Sandeep Shastri, "No Influence of National Issues in Tamil Nadu" *The Hindu*, 24th May, 2014.

Stoker, Gerry. "Governance as Theory: Five Propositions" in *Public Administration: A Reader*, (eds), Bidyut Chakrabarty and Mohit Bhattacharya, New Delhi: Oxford University Press, 2003.

Vora, Rajendra and Palshikar, Subas, *Indian Democracy: Meaning and Practices*, New Delhi: Sage Publications, 2004.

Weiner, Myron, *The Indian Paradox: Essays in Indian Politics*, New Delhi: Sage Publications, 1989.

Yadav, Yogendra and Palshikar, Suhas, "Ten Theses on State Politics in India" in Sandeep Shastri, K.C. Suri and Yogendra Yadav (eds.), *Electoral Politics in India in Indian States*, Delhi: Oxford University Press, 2009.

Index

Academic exercise, 2
Adult franchise, 2
Aggressive campaign, 19
Alagiri, 17, 47–48
All India Anna Dravida Munnetra Kazhagam (AIADMK), 6–7, 12, 15–20, 43–51, 55, 59–61, 79–80
  alliance, 16, 18
  camp, 16–17
  votes, 19
Alliance
  arithmetic, 16, 20
  formation, 50
American presidential election, 80
Animation skills, 71
Anti-Congress wave, 52
Anti-incumbent wave, 16, 21, 44–46, 55
Anti-party activities, 47
Arakkonam, 28
Assembly elections, 49

Bharatiya Janata Party (BJP), 6, 15, 18, 20, 43–45, 48–49, 52, 55, 59–60, 80
  alliance, 60
  leadership, 49
Black money, 43
By-election, 17, 20

Campaign meeting, 80
Casteist parties, 18
Civic culture, 12
Civil society organisations, 2, 4
Coalition government, 45
Communication skills, 77
Communist Party of India, 15
Community oriented schemes, 64
Computer culture, 76
Congress party, 50, 59
CPI, 16, 51
Cultural conditions, 8, 12–13
Cultural nationalism, 43

Dalit parties, 44
Democracy, 1–2, 4, 7–13, 41–42, 61, 76, 79, 81
  behavioural, 41
  consociational, 12
  electoral, 1, 4, 13
  institutional, 41
  operationalising, 1
  political, 41
  practice of, 12, 81
  social, 41
  western, 41
Democratic
  countries, 2–3, 41
  culture, 7–8, 79
  deficit, 1
  element, 7
  government, 63
  institutions, 41
  practices, 1, 79

regimes, 12–13
Democratic Progressive Alliance (DPA), 7, 15, 17–18
Democratization, 41
Desiya Murpokku Dravida Kazhagam (DMDK), 6, 18–19, 44, 47–50, 59–61, 80
Development indicators, 45
Development schemes, 4, 63–64, 72
Dravida Munnetra Kazhagam (DMK), 6–7, 11–12, 15–21, 43–52, 55, 59, 61, 79–80
alliance, 18, 20–21
perspective framework, 44
Dravidian parties, 6, 19, 44, 47–48, 50

Economic conditions, 66
Election
campaign, 45, 48, 55, 80
expenditure, 80
machinery, 3–4
management, 9, 17
period, 55
Election Commission, 7, 18, 42, 61
Electioneering, 11, 42–44, 48, 52, 59, 61, 80
Electoral
alliance, 45, 47, 51, 60, 79–80
contest, 4, 10
outcome, 8–9, 11–12
politics, 2–3
practices, 3–4
verdict, 19
victory, 19, 21
Electronic media strength, 19
Emergency, 11
Ethnic political parties, 6, 11

Fair governance, 3
Fairness, 3
Family grip, 46
First time voters, 60
Flagship programmes, 15
Focus group discussion, 64–66, 76
Formidable alliance, 44
Fractured verdict, 44

Gandhi, Rahul, 50–52, 55

Human development index, 42, 64

India Anna Dravida Munnetra Kazhagam, 12, 43
Indian National Congress, 6, 11–12, 14–20, 43–45, 47, 49–50, 52, 55, 59–61, 80
Indira Gandhi assassination, 11–12
Individual benefit schemes, 19
Infrastructure schemes, 19
Innovative politics, 79
Inseparable instrument, 70
Integrated Analysis, 55

Jayalalitha, 7, 17, 45–48, 52, 55, 60–61, 75, 79

Karunanidhi, 7, 16–17, 45, 47–48, 79
Krishnagiri, 29

Leadership, 6–7, 14–15, 17, 43, 59–60
effective, 11
strong, 11
weak, 11
Legislative Assembly elections, 21, 49, 59
Lok Sabha, 4, 6, 10, 12, 14–15, 17–18, 22–23, 41–44, 51, 59, 79–80
Low profile campaign, 50

Marginalised political parties, 48
Marumalarchi Dravida Munnetra Kazhagam (MDMK), 15–16, 18, 44, 48, 61, 80
Mayiladuturai, 36

Media
  representatives, 42
  rooms, 52
  survey, 20
Minimal democracy, 1–2, 4
Modi, Narendra, 45, 47, 50–51, 55, 60
Modi's wave, 48, 80
Money
  alliance, 50
  power, 10, 21, 59
  tickets, 50
Muslim parties and Dalit parties, 46

Nagapattinam, 36
National Democratic Alliance, 15
National Employment Guarantee Act, 15
National political parties, 43
New political culture, 79
Non-committed voters, 10, 20–21
Non-political organizations, 19
NREGA, 19–20

Open market cost, 11
Owning Development, 72

Parliamentary
  constituency, 25–40
  election, 8, 11
  politics, 51
Pattali Makkal Katchi (PMK), 15–16, 18, 44, 48, 61, 80
Peer group interaction, 70
Peravai, Kongu, 18–19
Periodic elections, 13
Personality development, 71
Political
  actions, 49
  activities, 7, 43
  formation, 80
  mobilizations, 2, 79
  orientations, 79
  regimes, 63, 72
  survival, 16
Poor governance, 43
Populist schemes, 20
Presidential election model, 43
Progressive activities, 15
Pro-poor schemes, 46
Provincial elections, 11

Rajya Sabha election, 51
Ramachandran, 79
Ramanathapuram, 38
Regional
  legislature, 8
  parties, 11
Regionalism, 43
Representative democracy, 2, 12, 41
Reservation, 72, 75
Rice politics, 11–12
Right to Information Act, 15
Ruling party, 19, 43, 49, 59–60, 64, 80
Rural vote banks, 20

Self-development, 71
Skill development, 71
Social conditions, 41
Social welfare programmes, 76
Socio-cultural
  conditions, 7
  institutions, 8
Socio-economic cultural conditions, 7
Stalin, K., 48
State autonomy, 43
State government machinery, 59
Sub-regional parties, 11

Telugu Desam, 20
Third World, 13
Trinamool Congress, 6

Unfair practices, 2, 4
United Progressive Alliance (UPA), 14–17, 43, 45, 50, 52

Untouchable parties, 61

Viduthalai Chiruthaikal Katchi (VCK), 16, 18
Vijayakanth, 49
Vote bank, 50, 61
Vote catching technique, 64
Voters sovereignty, 3

Welfare programmes, 15, 46, 76
Welfare schemes, 20, 43, 63–64
Win-win situation, 14
Work culture, 77